▶ **Democracy in Iran**

DOI: 10.1057/9781137330178

Other Palgrave Pivot titles

Mark Chou: Theorising Democide: Why and How Democracies Fail

David Levine: Pathology of the Capitalist Spirit: An Essay on Greed, Hope, and Loss

G. Douglas Atkins: Alexander Pope's Catholic Vision: "Slave to No Sect"

Frank Furedi: Moral Crusades in an Age of Mistrust: The Jimmy Savile Scandal

Edward J. Carvalho: Puerto Rico Is in the Heart: Emigration, Labor, and Politics in the Life and Work of Frank Espada

Peter Taylor-Gooby: The Double Crisis of the Welfare State and What We Can Do About It

Clayton D. Drinko: Theatrical Improvisation, Consciousness, and Cognition

Robert T. Tally Jr.: Utopia in the Age of Globalization: Space, Representation, and the World System

Benno Torgler and Marco Piatti: A Century of *American Economic Review*

Asha Sen: Postcolonial Yearning: Reshaping Spiritual and Secular Discourses in Contemporary Literature

Maria-Ionela Neagu: Decoding Political Discourse: Conceptual Metaphors and Argumentation

Ralf Emmers: Resource Management and Contested Territories in East Asia

Peter Conn: Adoption: A Brief Social and Cultural History

Niranjan Ramakrishnan: Reading Gandhi in the Twenty-First Century

Joel Gwynne: Erotic Memoirs and Postfeminism: The Politics of Pleasure

Ira Nadel: Modernism's Second Act: A Cultural Narrative

Andy Sumner and Richard Mallett: The Future of Foreign Aid: Development Cooperation and the New Geography of Global Poverty

Tariq Mukhimer: Hamas Rule in Gaza: Human Rights under Constraint

Khen Lampert: Meritocratic Education and Social Worthlessness

G. Douglas Atkins: Swift's Satires on Modernism: Battlegrounds of Reading and Writing

David Schultz: American Politics in the Age of Ignorance: Why Lawmakers Choose Belief over Research

G. Douglas Atkins: T.S. Eliot Materialized: Literal Meaning and Embodied Truth

Martin Barker: Live To Your Local Cinema: The Remarkable Rise of Livecasting

Michael Bennett: Narrating the Past through Theatre: Four Crucial Texts

Arthur Asa Berger: Media, Myth, and Society

Hamid Dabashi: Being a Muslim in the World

David Elliott: Fukushima: Impacts and Implications

Milton J. Esman: The Emerging American Garrison State

Kelly Forrest: Moments, Attachment and Formations of Selfhood: Dancing with Now

Steve Fuller: Preparing for Life in Humanity 2.0

Ioannis N. Grigoriadis: Instilling Religion in Greek and Turkish Nationalism: A "Sacred Synthesis"

Jonathan Hart: Textual Imitation: Making and Seeing in Literature

DOI: 10.1057/9781137330178

palgrave▸pivot

Democracy in Iran

▸

Ramin Jahanbegloo

Associated Professor, University of Toronto

DOI: 10.1057/9781137330178

First published 2013 by
PALGRAVE MACMILLAN

Palgrave Macmillan in the UK is an imprint of Macmillan Publishers Limited, registered in England, company number 785998, of Houndmills, Basingstoke, Hampshire RG21 6XS.

Palgrave Macmillan in the US is a division of St Martin's Press LLC, 175 Fifth Avenue, New York, NY 10010.

Palgrave Macmillan is the global academic imprint of the above companies and has companies and representatives throughout the world.

Palgrave® and Macmillan® are registered trademarks in the United States, the United Kingdom, Europe and other countries.

ISBN: 978–1–137–33018–5 EPUB
ISBN: 978–1–137–33017–8 PDF
ISBN: 978–1–137–33016–1 Hardback

A catalogue record for this book is available from the British Library.

A catalog record for this book is available from the Library of Congress.

www.palgrave.com/pivot

DOI: 10.1057/9781137330178

Contents

DOI: 10.1057/9781137330178

Acknowledgments

It is a pleasant duty to record my debts of gratitude to all those who have supported my research and the writing of this book. First and foremost thanks and respect to His Holiness the Dalai Lama for his teachings of nonviolence whose wisdom has had a profound impact on my work. I am also deeply grateful to the Political Science department at the University of Toronto and especially to its Chair, David Cameron. My interactions with peers and students at the University of Toronto since the year 2008 have allowed me to reflect upon and refine further some of the earlier arguments of this book. A special and grateful thanks to my assistant and friend, Richie Nojang Khatami, for his editing prowess, his good humor, and his hard work. I would also like to thank a number of people for their assistance in making this book possible. Many of these people have assisted me in the past few years in different manners: Saeed Rahnema, Farzin Vahdat, Melissa Williams, Elisabeth Young Bruehel, John Ralston Saul, Ashis Nandy, Sudhir Kakar, Michael Walzer, Rajmohan Gandhi, Bhikhu Parekh, Derek Allen, Noushin Ahmadi Khorasani, Nayereh Tohidi, Haideh Moghissi, Roberto Toscano, Giancarlo Bosetti, Nina Von Furstenberg, Fred Dallmayr, and members of the Agora Philosophical Forum. On a higher plane, I hope that members of my immediate family accept this book on nonviolence as a token of my sincere gratitude for all they have endured in the course of the last decade. Thank you to my mother, Khojasteh Kia, whose feedback I value the most in the world, and to my wife, whose love is precious, for helping

DOI: 10.1057/9781137330178

me see nonviolence through the eyes of Iranian women. Finally, I dedicate this book to my daughter, Afarin. I have been forever changed by the time I have been spending with her and watching the future of Iran from a front-row seat.

DOI: 10.1057/9781137330178

palgrave▶pivot

www.palgrave.com/pivot

Introduction

Abstract: *The modern history of Iran has been a narrative of violence in the form of conflicting discourses between the religious and the secular or between the modernists and the traditionalists. However, the ethical moment of nonviolence has become an ethical standard for the Iranian civil society against the absolutist nature of politics in contemporary Iran. The use of violence in contemporary Iranian politics has continuously diminished the power of those who use it. But the power of Iranian civil society has never grown out of the barrel of a gun. It has removed tyrants and changed social values by using its moral capital and practicing nonviolence.*

Jahanbegloo, Ramin. *Democracy in Iran.* Basingstoke: Palgrave Macmillan, 2013. DOI: 10.1057/9781137330178.

Few observers could deny that contemporary Iran, in light of its religious and political characteristics, is a country of violence. An observation and analysis of this violence, however, should not be extended to a rapid conclusion that Iranian society is alien and resistant to any nonviolent change. Since 1979, Iran's republican potentials and civic capacities have been overshadowed by the "Islamic theocratic mantle." For many analysts, Iran simply became a violent theocracy with no hope to forge a path toward nonviolent and democratic change. One of the central arguments of this book is that while Iran has been involved with politics of violence (especially during the last 100 years), inherited from its long and complex history, it would be absurd to consider nonviolence as an impossibility for Iran and Iranians. Moreover, it challenges a broader assumption about the inapplicability of what we can call a "Gandhian Moment" to Iran. This book seeks to show the potentialities and mechanisms of the "Gandhian Moment" in Iran, situating it firmly in the perspective of intellectual and social movements within the country, but also suggesting methods to understand the levels of violence in Iranian contemporary history. Therefore, in essence, this book is about an idea, namely nonviolence, and the obstacles to its development and consolidation. The central motif of this study is to refute the powerful political myth of violent emancipation in Iran, as if every step toward democracy in that country should be accompanied by the exclusion and murder of a religious, ethnic or intellectual minority. History bears witness, and everyday experience confirms, that the truth becomes a vehicle for violence as soon as it strays from the imperative of nonviolence.

George Santayana once said: "Those who cannot remember the past are condemned to repeat it."[1] Santayana was one to believe that the possibility of human progress was dependent on our human potential to retain our historical memory and build upon it. Yet, if we consider the generations of Iranians who have endured political violence and tyrannical rule, it seems probable that the opposite holds more truth in the historical record of the Iranian nation. It might come to us as a question why a nation which remembers its past, lives its past and honors its past is routinely repeating the repertoires of violence that constitute its legacy. After all, to remember an act of violence and to condemn it is to struggle against it, whether there are individuals who were directly or indirectly harmed by it or who directly or indirectly organized it. So, in the context of political violence in a country like Iran, how may remembering acts of violence make those affected more likely to repeat it? The answer to

DOI: 10.1057/9781137330178

this question may have to do with the fact that political violence is not a genetic concept but a political one which is subject to intergenerational fading of historical memory and deliberate forgetting. Needless to say, as memories are being passed down from generation to generation, they seem to lose elements of suffering that were endured in a group at a certain point in history. Therefore, the way societies internalize their collective memories of political violence and overcome it through an act of truthfulness becomes a salient feature in considering the possibility of nonviolent action among citizens. Simply put, one needs to explore the linkage between historical collective memory of violence and just how this figures in the violent practices of collective political action. The historical trauma of violence which is experienced by the Iranian collective memory seems to be rearticulated and reified onto and into Iranian political identity.

A dark cloud has hovered over Iranian political consciousness for hundreds of years, not to say for several thousand years. All through the ages, Iranian thinkers and mystics wondered whether anything mattered in a world where absolute violence was permitted. However, after the Iranian encounter with modernity Iranian intellectuals were forced to re-evaluate the idea of violence because of what this meant for modern politics. Therefore, they were confronted by the problem of justification and instrumentalization of violence, of how to act toward others in the context of absolute theologization or absolute secularization of the Iranian public sphere. More clearly, violence not only injured and annihilated them, but it also made them injure and annihilate others and, even worse, to betray their commitments to their own humanity. At this level, the ethical nature of consciousness among many Iranian intellectuals failed to oppose the historical course of violence. Iranian history said: violence. Intellectual consciousness rebounded and said: violence. Accordingly, Iranian intellectuals have always been face-to-face with the modern predicament of violence. It is within this predicament that a motivated calling to mind of the historical remembrance of violence in Iranian history became a condition for new forms of violence.

Taken all together, the modern history of Iran has been a narrative of violence in the form of conflicting discourses between the religious and the secular or between the modernists and the traditionalists. As Iran encountered modernity, these discourses have competed and at different times, one or the other has prevailed, significantly changing the course of Iran's history. Each one of these changes linked for a short

DOI: 10.1057/9781137330178

period of time the history of violence in modern Iran with the history-to-be-made of nonviolence. True, nonviolence in Iran has always been the call of a few; but it has always appeared as the wish of all. After all, nonviolent action has always been a situation of "new beginning" in Iran where people need to confront the cycle of violence and hatred that often obscures democratic efforts and closes the doors to reconciliation and solidarity. The recent unrest in Iran is about a much deeper crisis taking place in the Iranian power structure and it is likely to bring about a major transformation of the Islamic Republic. What seems evident in this particular crisis is that a whole series of ideological beliefs and political institutions inherited from the revolution of 1979 are now put into question. Among these, we find the cherished belief that the Islamic revolution removed tyranny and established a system of social justice. However, the regime's conduct in the past year has presented serious challenges to its own political institutions while undermining its republican principles by granting no legitimacy to the judgment of the Iranian public sphere. Regardless of whether there was significant fraud in the presidential elections, the architects of the political establishment who believed that the system allowed scope of reform and change find themselves increasingly face-to-face with an authoritarian structure that uses extreme violence to ensure its political survival. The exceptional concentration of power and uncontested control of violence by a few institutions in Iran has led some scholars to describe the Iranian system as a "sultanistic" institutional structure.[2] However, this concentration of power to make and unmake rules and laws denotes a permanent exercise of absolute sovereignty rather than alluding to "a state of emergency."

Such an argument can be traced back to Hobbes' and Schmitt's theories of sovereignty and legitimacy. Carl Schmitt's work draws heavily on Thomas Hobbes' understanding of the obedience/protection principle. For both, sovereignty resides where there is power to provide protection from enemies in return for obedience. According to John McCormick, "As Carl Schmitt puts it, '*protego ergo obligo*' is the '*cogito ergo sum*' of the state."[3] Carl Schmitt himself voices his admiration for Hobbes for having grasped this principle as the foundation of sovereignty and legitimacy and openly acknowledges his own debt to Hobbes on this crucial point. For both Hobbes and Schmitt the idea of security is of paramount importance. The sovereignty must be absolute, unlimited and irrevocable because such unmitigated power would provide the greatest level of security. According to Peter Steinberger, "There appears to be no such

DOI: 10.1057/9781137330178

notion of accountability, regular or otherwise. The original contractors who compose the authorizing entity have created an instrumental entity – a sovereign – that seems not to be accountable at all. For as we all know, the Hobbesian sovereign has complete authority over the commonwealth's citizens. To be sure, Hobbes also says that the sovereign has a perfect right to try to overcome any and all resistance. The citizen's right to disobey does not compromise the sovereign's right to enforce obedience."[4] The citizen cannot decide to obey this law and to disobey that; there can be no such thing as civil disobedience; there can be no division of sovereignty, no checks and balances, no external constraints on the sovereign's actions. As David van Mill notes in quoting Hobbes, "The key is to safeguard peace 'and this is intended should be done, not by care applied to individuals, further than their protection from injuries when they shall complain, but by a general providence, contained in public instruction, both of doctrine and example, and in the making and executing of good laws, to which individuals may apply their own cases.'"[5] Hence the task for the sovereign is to bring the subjects into obedience: "these rights have to be diligently and truly taught, because they cannot be maintained by any civil law or terror of legal punishment."[6]

Hobbes thus plainly recognizes and celebrates the virtues of coercive power, and adopts with enthusiasm an attitude of pragmatic absolutism. In this case, the sovereign's status is not a perpetually open question. To obey an absolute sovereign is not a matter of exception, because as Schmitt says "The sovereign is he who decides on the exception."[7] As has been said, "It is a disturbingly 'realistic' view of politics which subordinates *de jure* authority to *de facto* power."[8] The law, in this case, is made by the one who has power and not the one who possesses the truth. So, it is precisely the exceptional power of the sovereign that defines the essence of politics and not the necessity of an immediate response to an unforeseen event. As such, the essence of the political in case of absolute sovereignty is what can be decided on and become legal through pure violence. This means that the whole legal order is based on the sovereign judgment and decision and not concretized in a norm. In other words, the absolute sovereign constantly defines true politics as the defense of the existing order against the overturning of established order. This implies that there is a permanent tension between the structure of politics in a violent order and the potential for the "political" as an agency to assert itself through the emergence of a competing notion of order and social organization.[9]

DOI: 10.1057/9781137330178

During the last three decades the Islamic regime, its political and judicial structures have dominated all the spheres of Iranian life by imposing a high degree of violence. Despite this extreme violence and all the dangers that it implicated, women's rights activists, intellectuals and students groups found a voice in the Iranian public sphere and worked constantly to gain their freedom of expression and other basic rights. Principled preference for nonviolence among all these civil society groups revealed a curiously persistent method of interacting with the prevailing authoritarian norms, values and laws. Therefore, nonviolence was employed by Iranian civil society with complete confidence and to its greatest moral advantage. Violence, on the other hand, was viewed both as immoral and impractical since it continued to generate new and more complicated problems than the ones it aimed to solve. It generated a legacy of negative sentiments that perpetuated conflict rather than peace. Interestingly, in today's Iran, nonviolence is not only considered as a strategy for wining a conflict, but also as a mentality that makes it impossible for new arbitrary rulers to control the lives of Iranian citizens. An arbitrary ruler's vulnerability to nonviolent resistance is rarely visible to those who underestimate the moral and political force of nonviolence. Iranian people have an advantage in their nonviolent struggle that many other countries in the region lack: they have democratic and nonviolent memories to draw upon. The Constitutional Revolution of 1906, the Mossadeq movement and the Revolution of 1979 exemplify many of the nonviolent attributes which can appeal to Iranian civil society.

Looking back, one can argue that nonviolent action in many instances of these historical events has been a means of achieving change and the first line of defense of democracy. Four generations of Iranians had to use nonviolent methods to show how morally different and how spiritually creative they were in comparison with the arbitrary leaders who oppressed them. As such, nonviolent sanctions have been far more frequent and widespread in Iranian contemporary history than usually supposed. They continue to be crucial elements of history-making struggles in Iran today. Many continue to believe that violence is the ultimate form of politics in a country like Iran. Told that way, Iranian contemporary history would reinforce a terrible fallacy: that only violent action can overcome a violent regime; that democracy can only be gained by force of arms. If that were true, a nonviolent politician like Mossadeq could not have come to dominate the Iranian political landscape. However, one important point to recognize is that though

DOI: 10.1057/9781137330178

the potential for democratization of Iran was present in figures like Mossadeq and in many Iranian nonviolent movements, all the major nation-changing popular movements for self-rule ended tragically in violence and in a new arbitrary rule. The more was given to Iranian tyrants, the more they fortified themselves and the more they asked for obedience. But violence is like nonviolence in at least two ways: it does not always succeed, and it operates by identifying an opponent's weakest points. A political regime seeking to practice more control will often resort to extreme violence. However, violence is not a function of fate; it can fail and it usually does.

Never in the past hundred years did the Iranian people possess any military advantage over the regimes they confronted. But this military weakness never dissuaded Iranians from rising against different forms of injustice. The nonviolent action they took had a moral value and legitimacy in overcoming the violence of a government that had lost all moral and political legitimacy. At each crossroad of history it undermined the regime's claim to moral legitimacy and it diminished its political control over people's fates. In her incomparable essay, "On Violence," Hannah Arendt argues that violence is "utterly incapable" of creating power – that "The danger of violence, even if it moves consciously in a non-extremist framework of short-term goals, will always be that the means overwhelm the end. If goals are not achieved rapidly, the result will be not merely defeat but the introduction of the practice of violence into the whole body politic."[10] Arendt explains perfectly how violence diminishes the power of those who use it. This has always been the case in Iranian contemporary history. But the power of Iranian civil society has never grown out of the barrel of a gun. It has removed tyrants and changed social values by using its moral capital and practicing nonviolence. The uncertainty of the final outcome of political struggle in Iran today should lead us to underline the primacy of nonviolent means over the contingency of ends. Today, the Gandhian moment of nonviolence has become an ethical standard around the world, and with a few exceptions like the Islamic theocracy in Iran, its enemies are gone. More than a hundred years after the Constitutional Revolution of 1906, Iranian people are still in quest of a social covenant through which they can acquire and practice public freedom. This is their hope. But it is also their faith in the future of Iran. With this faith they will be able to work together, to struggle together and to stand up for freedom together. But it is only when they shall take no part in violence and shall be ready to suffer every persecution that

DOI: 10.1057/9781137330178

their disavowal of violence will bring them a freedom that will ring from the snow-capped heights of Mount Alborz.

Notes

1   George Santayana, *Life of Reason: Vol.1,* New York: Scribner, 1953, p.397.
2   Akbar Ganji, "The Struggle Against Sultanism," *Journal of Democracy* Vol. 16, no. 4 (2005): 38–51.
3   Quoted in John P. McCormick, "Fear, Technology, and the State: Carl Schmitt, Leo Strauss, and the Revival of Hobbes in Weimar and National Socialist Germany," *Political Theory* Vol. 22, no. 4 (November 1994): 619–652.
4   Peter Steinberger, "Hobbes, Rousseau and the Modern Conception of the State," *Journal of Politics* Vol. 70, no. 3 (2008): p. 604.
5   David van Mill, "Hobbes and the Limits of Freedom," paper prepared for the Australasian Political Studies Association, October 4–6, 2000.
6   Thomas Hobbes, *Leviathan*, ed. C.B. Macpherson. London: Penguin Books, 1968, pp. 376–377.
7   See Carl Schmitt, *Political Theology*, Chicago, Illinois: University of Chicago Press, 2006.
8   S. Parvez Manzoor, "The Sovereignty of the Political: Carl Schmitt and the Nemesis of Liberalism," see http://evans-experientialism.freewebspace.com/carlschmitte.htm.
9   Peter Steinberger, "Hobbes, Rousseau and the Modern Conception of the State," *Journal of Politics* Vol. 70, no. 3 (2008): p. 598.
10 Hannah Arendt, *On Violence*. New York: Harvest Books, 1970, pp. 153–155.

DOI: 10.1057/9781137330178

Part I
Iran: The Anguished Odyssey of Democracy

▶

DOI: 10.1057/9781137330178

1

Iran: A Century of Undemocratic Violence

Abstract: *The history of 20th century Iran is dominated by reoccurring episodes of civic struggles in the face of three successive authoritarian regimes – Qajar, Pahlavi and the Islamic Republic. This century also saw two defining moments in Iranian history: the Constitutional Revolution 1906 and the Islamic Revolution of 1979. Although these revolutions were preceded by violent and nondemocratic regimes, they created positive and concrete consequences. The first revolution was significant because it ushered in a protracted period of modernization, culminating in the implementation of liberal reforms. And while the Islamic Revolution has seen an unprecedented centralization of the state, it has led to the strengthening of civil society, opening the door for viable democratic movements.*

Jahanbegloo, Ramin. *Democracy in Iran*. Basingstoke: Palgrave Macmillan, 2013. DOI: 10.1057/9781137330178.

DOI: 10.1057/9781137330178

Much of the contemporary history of Iran is the story of clashes between aspirations for freedom and obstacles to democracy. Starting from Iran's 1906 Constitutional Revolution to the Islamic Revolution of 1979, contemporary Iranian politics has been the scene of multiple sociopolitical efforts and civic struggles to place limits on the despotic sovereignties of the Qajar and Pahlavi dynasties. The goal of each of these two revolutions was to limit state authority and assure political liberties enshrined in law. However, in both cases, popular aspirations for democracy, social justice and the rule of law were obstructed by the enduring violence of traditionalism and authoritarianism inscribed in the political structures of Iran and Iranian political culture. This said, despite the short and momentary successes of nonviolent actions in contemporary Iran, there has been a permanent subjection of the Iranian civic actors to the systematic and oppressive violence of the political establishment. From the second half of the 19th century until the present day, members of the Iranian elite, a certain number of Iranian guilds and merchants and dissident elements of the Iranian Shi'ite clergy, have been constantly in conflict with various political regimes in power. The authoritarian character of the three Iranian successive regimes – Qajar, Pahlavi and Islamic Republic – pushed different categories of Iranian society to look for diverse strategies of resistance in order to find freedom and security. Though the ideas of reform and modernity started in late-19th century Iran among the aristocratic and elite classes, it gradually extended to other social classes, who became familiar with the West and were interested in entering the public sphere. That is to say, the intellectual encounters with the West, which started with the first efforts of the Qajar prince Abbas Mirza to modernize the Iranian army and the policy of centralization and rationalization of the state bureaucracy inaugurated and pursued by Naser ad-Din Shah's prime minister, Mirza Taqi Khan Amir Kabir after the military defeats of Persia at Russian hands in 1812 and 1828, made their ways from the upper classes to ordinary civic actors in Iran who acclaimed and accepted the modern idea of a constitutional government in 1906. Moreover, the awareness of the need for a less cruel and more just political system came through the Iranian public sphere itself. The spreading of ideas such as "moderation" (*itidal*) which became a popular concept helped a new era of political culture to emerge in Iran. However, this advent of nonviolent and moderate political vocabulary in Iranian public sphere was accompanied by the growth of authoritarianism and its onslaught against civil society.

DOI: 10.1057/9781137330178

In general, next and in opposition to grass-roots democratic and nonviolent experiences in Iran, it is possible to identify different phases of violent state-domination throughout the 20th century. This political domination was not a natural process of Iranian society, but a top-down project ordered and applied by different authoritarian regimes in Iran. The peripheralization of the Iranian society as a result of Iran's dangerous and uncertain buffer-state position between imperial Russia and British Empire led to three experiences of authoritarian state formation from above. The first time was between 1921 and 1941 under Reza Shah which was essentially marked by the establishment of a modernist state. The second attempt occurred during the reign of Mohammad Reza Shah, between 1953 and 1977, and manifested itself as a techno-bureaucratic program that included land reform, industrialization, and royal-patrimonial rule. The third experience from 1979 to the present day is illustrated by a theocratic and clan-oriented regime which has systematically abolished secular criteria and promoted Islamic fundamentalist values in Iran. As a matter of fact in three cases, but more especially in the latter, the governing class based its ideological project on the violent apparatus of the authoritarian state in order to usher in a modernization process from above. As a result from 1921 to 2011 the Iranian society shifted from a tribalist and rural order to a more urban and middle class structure. But rapid urbanization and the development of urban workers and the middle class in Iran happened without fundamental changes in the nature of the political system. Paradoxically, the royal-nationalist projects of the first and second Pahlavi regimes and the revolutionary Islamic political ideology of the present Iranian theocracy each created a vacuum which was filled by Iranian civil society and its sociological actors. In the case of Iran, civil society can be described as a voluntary zone of societal interconnectedness separate from the structures of state and family and containing a wide variety of cultural associations, advocacy groups, labor unions, ethnic associations, student groups, women's right movements, intellectual spheres and alternative youth circles. Though nonviolent initiatives have often been related to civil society development in Iran, the nature of modernization itself and the centralization of the Iranian state has been a way of strengthening the erratic movement of the Iranian civil society. As such, despite the fact that it gives an impression of instability and uncertainty, the evolution of the Iranian state-society relations in the past 80 years has created real opportunities for inaugurating a viable democratic movement. The

DOI: 10.1057/9781137330178

development of nonviolent ideals and principles and the expansion of civil rights, occur not overnight but over decades. Historically, Iranian society's experiences with democracy have been intense and widespread. Revolutionary upheavals, urban riots, anti-government guerilla insurgencies, coup d'états, state oppression have had enduring impacts on the Iranian society. These events, along with the gradual transformation of Iranian civil society have reshaped the foundation of Iran's political culture. Thus the roots of today's nonviolent public initiatives in Iran can be found in the increasing disenchantment of various sections of Iranian society like intellectuals, youth and women groups with the palpable political handicaps and moral weaknesses of successive ailing states in contemporary Iran.

Twentieth-century Iran started with one revolution and ended with another. Those who hailed the Constitutional Revolution of 1906 and were inspired by its republican ideals found themselves a decade later confronted with political disappointment and disintegration of Iran. The coup of February 21, 1921 which brought Reza Khan, the commander of the Cossack Brigade, to power put an end to the post–World War I chaotic environment in Iran. "Critics of the Pahlavi state and Reza Khan in particular argue that he was the solution to Britain's problems in Iran after the failure of the Anglo-Persian Agreement and Britain's need for strong government in Iran."[1] While in retrospect Reza Khan's rise to power may appear to some as a British conspiracy, it certainly was confirmation of a savior to Iranian nationalists and especially the secular elites. As such, "In the early years of Reza Khan's rise to power, he was seen as a modernizing reformer who could give Iran national unity and restore the country's pride and independence. The reformist intelligentsia rallied behind Reza Khan, perceiving him as a stabilizing, nationalist force."[2] Nationalism and state centralization went hand in hand during Reza Shah's reign. Drawing on the necessity of Iran's discovery of its classical past, the ideological and political manifestations of Iranian nationalism were articulated within the formation of a modern nation-state and through loyalty to traditional monarchy. As pointed out by two Iranian political historians "It is important to note that Reza Khan's emphasis on institution-building was able to gain support because it evoked memories of the state among the Iranian people. The legacy of monarchical rule in Iran dating back to the Safavid period (1501–1722) had given Iranians a keen sense of the rights and duties of central authority, as well as the style and language of government. Reza

DOI: 10.1057/9781137330178

Khan's promise of a modern state would resonate with a broad segment of the Iranian population through this memory...."[3] But Reza Shah's national project for reconstruction of Iran produced at the same time a strong modernizing impetus which distanced itself from aristocratic and religious institutions. It especially found allies among secular elites and reformers like Mohammad Ali Foroughi, Ali Akbar Davar and Abdul Hussein Teymourtache, who accepted to help Reza Shah with his project of modern state-building. Foroughi belonged to a generation of Iranian intellectuals, who, thanks to the Constitutional Revolution of 1906, were able to participate more actively in the political life of the country. The hope and goal of Foroughi was to create suitable conditions for the implementation of modern and liberal principles in Iran, by concentrating his efforts on "reforms from above." Like most of the modernist intellectuals of his generation, Foroughi considered Reza Shah as the charismatic leader who would put an end to the chaotic situation of post–World War I Iran. To realize such an aim, Foroughi supported the extensive program of reform instituted by Reza Shah during his two premierships. Yet Foroughi's political career started many years before Reza Shah's rise to power, with the foundation of the first official Freemason's lodge in Iran in 1908, called "Le Reveil de l'Iran," where he held the rank of Grand Master. For Foroughi, as for Mirza Malkum Khan before him, freemasonry was an institution dedicated to striving to spread ideals of modernity in Iran through universalization and promotion of Western principles of freedom, education and secularism. Foroughi's defense of liberal values and ideals was closely related to his empathy for the philosophical norms of the Western civilization. It is worth mentioning here that Foroughi, while being a fabulous commentator of the Persian literary heritage, was also an attentive reader of the works of Plato and Aristotle. In 1922 Foroughi published his most famous and celebrated philosophical work entitled *Seyr-e Hekmat Dar Urupa* (The Course of Philosophy in Europe). When Foroughi started this book, he had intended it to be a translation of Rene Descartes' *Discours de la Methode*, but after translating this work into Persian he realized that this treatise would not be complete unless proper attention was given to the philosophical developments...prior to the time of Descartes. Therefore, he included a long introduction in which he briefly discussed the historical development of philosophy beginning in ancient Greece and going up to the time of Descartes. The 1941 edition of this book saw a considerable expansion containing the historical

DOI: 10.1057/9781137330178

development of philosophy in Europe starting in the beginning of the 19th century and ending in the early 20th century.

Foroughi's interest in Descartes as the founding father of modern philosophy and a great philosopher of subjectivity was not without any reason. For Foroughi, Descartes was the initiator of the Enlightenment and to him the Enlightenment meant essentially ridding human individuals from self-imposed bondage to authority and conferring on each individual the responsibility to make personally informed judgments. In Foroughi's mind the Enlightenment was supposed to emancipate mankind and autonomy as opposed to authority and was to be the hallmark of a new culture. According to Foroughi, in order for the Enlightenment to prevail in Iran two conditions must come together. Not only is it necessary that the constraining forces in society should be introduced in the shape of institutions, but also it is necessary that other types of institutions should be introduced to oversee, as well as improve, the performances of the former type of institutions. Together, these furnish the sufficient condition for the establishment and maintenance of equilibrium in a political society, thus laying the ground for the ideals of the Enlightenment to flourish. What comes across Foroughi's writings is an absolute belief in the idea of progress and a discussion on the separation of powers and the rights of the people under a liberal constitution. First and foremost in Foroughi's thought is the idea of inevitability of progress and the fact that progress in the West has been entirely responsible for a liberal re-organization of the social, economic and political spheres. The secret of this re-organization, which in Foroughi's opinion is the main cause of Western civilization's scientific and technological advances and achievements, lies in devising a system for administration in every field that is based on an evolutionary process. It is clear that Foroughi's main goal was to introduce the Iranian youth to modern rationality and to make them think about their own peripheral destiny. In fact, it seems that intellectuals such as Foroughi hoped to bring about the necessary reforms in Iran by educating Iranian youth to the philosophical outlook of modernity founded on a wide range of knowledge on politics, economics, science and culture. Foroughi knew perfectly that modernity began with the emphasis on reason and the philosophical self-assertion of the subject.

Liberal and reformist intellectuals like Foroughi presented the intellectual capital behind Reza Shah's brute force. But what made their position increasingly untenable in the new Pahlavi state were not only

DOI: 10.1057/9781137330178

the inordinately suspicious nature of the Shah, which caused him to mistrust his close collaborators, but also his power, greed and dictatorial ambitions which fuelled rebellion and discord among different Iranian social categories.

Reza Shah's secular program of modernization, however, created a great deal of discontent and exclusion among the ulama and the traditional bazaar. The ulama "began to agitate against the changes in the dress code which promoted the wearing of the Pahlavi hat and short jacket, especially among government employees, as well as the reforms in the judiciary..."⁴ Thus in the years 1926–1927 waves of protests against Reza Shah's state reforms engulfed a number of Iranian cities like Tehran, Isfahan and Shiraz. "As the Pahlavi state became increasingly characterized by arbitrary rule, Iranians found themselves facing a Faustian choice between developmentalism and democracy, an end that would not benefit Iran and the Pahlavi regime. Reza Shah's failure was in how he achieved his success, and in forcing Iranians to choose between the ideals of development and democracy rather than creating an institutional framework that could fuse the quest for both."⁵ The forced unveiling of women in the late 1920s in Iran stirred protests and anti-Reza Shah sentiments among the ulama and more traditional elements of Iranian society. However, not all members of the religious establishment protested so actively. Some, such as the pre-eminent religious leader of the time, the Grand Ayatulla 'Abd al-Karim Ha'iri, embraced political quietism. Others, such as the modernist theologian, Mirza Riza Quli Shari'at Sagalaji, probably the most important religious thinker of the period, urged the ulama to abandon their reactionary stance and make use of *ijtihad* in reinterpreting and modernizing Islam."⁶ However, the discomfort and resentment created by Reza Shah's authoritarian and modernist policies were not directly responsible for the downfall of the first Pahlavi regime. Reza Shah's downfall came not from within and because of the authoritarian measure of his state, but from outside and as a challenge posed by the Allied forces during World War II. "The British saw Reza Shah as aggravating their vulnerabilities, especially when, having rebuffed by the US, he returned to Germany for security against USSR."⁷ The invasion of Iran in August 1941 activated the capitulation of Reza Shah and the collapse of his state. As such, the coercive state that symbolized Reza Shah's authoritarian rule was defeated by a greater violence, that of the Allied army, and paved the way to future political clashes and crises.

DOI: 10.1057/9781137330178

The occupation of Iran by Allied forces and the abdication of Reza Shah followed by the access to power of his son, Mohammad Reza Shah Pahlavi, left the Iranian public space open to factionalism and political instability. "Four political blocs were formed: one consisted of the big landowners who also represented certain commercial sectors, together with the high aristocracy of the sword and the religious aristocracy, which also included top-level officials in the administration. The second bloc was formed by the Marxists and Socialists. The third was the bloc of Nationalists and Liberals (Azadikhahan) of every stamp, gathered around Mossadeq. Finally, the fourth bloc comprised the Bazaris as well as middle-level white collar workers and outsiders (Ayatollah Kashani)."[8] Given the circumstances of the time and the young Shah's lack of political experience to deal appropriately with the Cold War paradigm it was difficult for him to gather his autocratic powers as his father had done in the 1920s. The Shah's youthful enthusiasm for his father's reforms were not enough to provide him with the necessary political maturity to deal with the upcoming crises. The young Shah is portrayed by some Iranian historians like Homa Katouzian as a "timid as well as intimated man, suffering from a basic sense of insecurity which was further exacerbated by his own superficiality as well as lack of knowledge and wisdom because he felt dwarfed by them. He enjoyed the company of women and of sycophants but did not trust them. He was acutely worried about a foreign (mainly British) plot to dislodge him, and he therefore took extreme care not to displease them. He had an idealistic view of the United States, not just as a potential patron and benefactor, but also as the best and most advanced society on earth. He wished to increase his personal hold over the country, but lacked courage and decisiveness, and hoped that others would do it for him."[9] Thus Mohammad Reza Shah's efforts to inherit the strong will and the brute force of his father proved premature. The fact is that more than his father the Shah had to confront, during his political life, four big challenges, each bringing him to the edge of depression or downfall. The first significant challenge for the Shah was to come in the Azerbaijan crisis in 1946. Supported by the Soviet troops in the province, the Democratic Party of Azerbaijan led by Pishevari announced the establishment of an autonomous state. Totally unfamiliar with the art of diplomacy and incapable of solving the problem, the Shah turned to his Prime Minister Ahmad Qavam who granted Stalin an oil concession in the north of Iran if they accepted to withdraw their troops from Tabriz within six weeks. With the Soviet troops out of Azerbaijan and

DOI: 10.1057/9781137330178

the collapse of the separatist movement, the Shah visited Tabriz in 1947 and celebrated what became "the liberation of Azerbaijan" as his own personal victory. "The immediate political impact of the reoccupation of Azerbaijan was the re-emergence of the Shah as a central player in the Iranian political process. Far from willing to operate within strictly defined if highly constrained constitutional parameters, the young Shah was anxious to make his mark and to portray himself as a worthy successor to his father, with whom unfavorable comparisons were regularly being made."[10] Not having a personal hold on political power, the Shah had to confront his second challenge which this time threatened the very foundations of the regime. Unlike the Shah, who was completely alien to the liberal values of the Constitutional Revolution of 1906, Mohamad Mossadeq was fast emerging as a popular and constitutional leader among Iranian crowd. It was Ali Razmara's assassination on March 7, 1951 by a member of the Islamic fundamentalist group, Feda'iyan-I Islam, which acted as a catalyst for Mossadeq's rise to power and the oil nationalization. Razamara had replaced Ali Mansur, who himself became the Prime Minister shortly after the resignation of Ahmad Qavam in 1947. With Razmara's assassination and the political crisis that faced the regime, the Shah decided to dissolve the Majlis (Iranian parliament) in order to seize control of the country. However, due to the miscalculations of the Shah and the British and the weaknesses of Hossein Ala, a compromise candidate for premiership, the Majlis asked Mossadeq to step forward and take full responsibility as Prime Minister. "Binding himself to the principle of nationalization, Mossadeq insisted that his acceptance be predicated on the ratification of the nationalization law, which the Majlis dutifully approved on 28 April 1951, followed by the Senate the following day. The Shah, much to the consternation of the British Government, immediately signed the new law."[11]

Arguably, Mossadeq's victory was that of the Iranian people, who were eager to see the true application of constitutionalism and nationalism in Iran. Conscious of his popularity and power and British stranglehold on Iran's sterling assets and banned export of goods to Iran Mossadeq decided to settle the Anglo-Iranian oil dispute by taking the matter to the International Court of Justice at The Hague in July 1951 and to challenge the British on the legality of the oil nationalization. The court found in Iran's favor, but the dispute between Iran and the AIOC remained unsettled and Iranian economy continued to suffer from the loss of foreign exchange and oil revenues. "The government was left with little

DOI: 10.1057/9781137330178

choice but to balance its budget deficits by means of various domestic fiscal and monetary policies, including an increase in the fiduciary note issue...Finally, the government's tough austerity measures inevitably led to a fall in public welfare. It was the government's great popularity which enabled it to take such unpopular measures without provoking a backlash of public opinion against itself."[12] Meanwhile, Mossadeq's victory on the oil issue created more frictions between him and the Shah. In the summer of 1952, the Shah refused Mossadeq's demand for the power to appoint the Minister of War. As a result, Mossadeq resigned but after three days of popular riot in the streets of Tehran, the Shah was forced to reappoint Mossadeq to head the government. This incident, followed by the Prime Minister's support in the lower house of the Majlis on August 3, 1953 to organize a plebiscite for the dissolution of the legislative body, made the Americans and the British to admit the fact that no compromise with Mossadeq was possible. Fear of a Tudeh Party takeover and the spread of communism in Iran, resulted in the proposal for a joint Anglo-American operation, and code-named Operation Ajax, to overthrow Mossadeq. In accord with the British–American plan, on August 13 the Shah issued a decree dismissing Mossadeq and appointing General Zahedi as Prime Minister. Mossadeq refused to step down and the Shah decided suddenly to flee the country and to go to Rome. However, after four days of riot the pro-Shah army units and street crowds defeated Mossadeq's forces on August 19, 1953. Mossadeq was arrested, put on trial and sentenced to three years' imprisonment. His minister of foreign affairs, Hosain Fatemi, was sentenced to death and executed. Mossadeq remained under house arrest in his village outside Tehran until the time of his death in 1967.

The coup d'état of 1953 did not put an end to the myth of Mossadeq in Iranian political memory. Neither did it end the nonviolent agenda of Iranian civil society which remained loyal to the message of the Constitutional Revolution of 1906. The dominant social and political conditions of the post-coup d'état Iran in the 1960s and 1970s was the consolidation of the Shah's power based on control and use of oil revenues. "By all external accounts, the Shah's position was in the ascendant by the late 1950s. He had successfully managed his relationship with the traditional classes, had terminated the military government in Tehran and established SAVAK...He constantly stressed his constitutional credentials and repeatedly emphasized that freedom and democracy existed in Iran."[13] However, the Shah and his monarchist technocrats came to

DOI: 10.1057/9781137330178

consider civil rights and economic development as mutually exclusive goals for Iran and gradually replaced the political maturity and moral integrity of Constitutional elite with a technocratic and bureaucratic spirit. "The culture of technocracy, however, also led to the cultural alienation of the state and the Pahlavi elite. The focus on development in the absence of competitive politics made the bureaucratic elite immune to demands from below. This also enabled them to more freely embrace Western culture and attitudes, which accentuated the divide between state and society. This eventually made it difficult for the Shah to convince Iranians of the merits and promises of his development agenda."[14] The first expression of the Shah's developmentalist program was the so-called Shah's White Revolution which involved a series of reforms such as land redistribution, emancipation of women and profit sharing plans for workers. It is well-known to readers of Iranian history that these reforms occurred at a time when the Kenedy administration was not only trying to contain communist domination of Iran, but also to help make the Shah popular among Iranian population. "Most American officials agreed that if the Shah did not initiate reforms, whatever the method, he eventually would be overthrown."[15] Surprisingly, the Shah's "white" reforms created a new challenge for the Shah's regime, which this time ended with his downfall 15 years later in 1979. The Shah had to confront a new alliance between the clergy and the bazaar. Though in 1953 the ulama had supported the Shah against Mossadeq, fearing the rise of communism in Iran, the Shah's reforms pushed the more radical and nonquietist elements of the Iranian clergy to turn against the whole program of the White Revolution and the referendum which was suggested by the Shah in January 1963. Among these a little-known cleric named Rouhollah Khomeini discredited the referendum as illegal and formulated an attack against the USA and Israel. "In Qum, anti-government sentiment was manifested in protest and prayer, which instigated a government response in the form of a commando attack on the Faiziyya school, where Khomeini taught, on 22 March 1963. One student was killed and many others injured. Khomeini moved instantly to take the advantage and discredit the government as much as possible, designating it to be a 'usurper' and *ipso facto* illegitimate."[16] The arrest of Khomeini on June 5, 1963 was followed by a series of urban unrest in Qum, Tehran, Shiraz and Mashhad which undermined directly the legitimacy of the Shah's regime. Khomeini was finally released in April 1964, but he continued criticizing the government as being anti-Islamic.

DOI: 10.1057/9781137330178

He made a famous speech in October 1964 against the $200 million loan from the USA for arms purchases. "Our dignity has been trampled underfoot" expressed Khomeini. "The dignity of Iran has been destroyed... They have reduced the Iranian people to a level lower than of an American dog. If someone runs over a dog belonging to an American, he will be prosecuted. But if an American cook runs over the Shah, the head of state, no one will have the right to interfere with him. Why? Because they wanted a loan and America demanded this in return."[17] Khomeini was arrested and sent to exile in Turkey few days after his speech. One year later he was authorized to change his place of exile to Najaf, where he remained until the Revolution of 1978–1979. With Khomeini in Najaf, his students and other radical clerics were actively engaged in the struggle against the Shah's regime. In the 15 years that followed the events of 1963 and Khomeini's exile, the Shah's regime faced a serious political crisis that the repressive of the SAVAK could not help to dissipate. Once again, despite the efforts of his advisors to channel the social malaise in mid-1970s, the Shah was confronted with the drop in oil revenues and economic cutbacks. On the other hand, the political vacuum, left in Iranian public sphere by the absence of alliance between secular forces and lack of negotiations between the Shah and the more Liberal elements, produced an opportunity for the religious elements and fundamentalists to control the political scene. It is important to note that the opposition to the Shah, either leftist or Islamist, set itself not only on the revolutionary ground but also on a violent one. However, it is interesting to note that though the opposition to the Pahlavi regime was not focused on the concept of nonviolence, the revolution itself unfolded as a nonviolent movement over a period of 18 months.

Notes

1   Ali M. Ansari, *Modern Iran: The Pahlavis and After*, 2nd edition, Pearson Education Limited, Essex 2007, p. 32.

2   M.R. Ghods, "Iranian Nationalism and Reza Shah," *Middle Eastern Studies* Vol. 27, no. 1 (1991): 37.

3   Ali Gheissari and Vali Nasr, *Democracy in Iran: History and the Quest for Liberty*, Oxford University Press, Oxford 2006, p. 37.

4   Ansari, *Modern Iran*, p. 57.

5   Gheissari and Nasr, *Democracy in Iran*, p. 43.

DOI: 10.1057/9781137330178

6   Stephanie Cronin, (ed.), *The Making of Modern Iran: State and Society under Riza Shah, 1921–1941*, Routledge, London 2003, p. 188.

7   Simon Davis, *Contested Space: Anglo-American Relations in the Persian Gulf, 1939–1947*, Martinus Nijhoff Publishers, Leiden 2009, p. 68.

8   Mehdi Mozzafari, "Why the Bazaar Rebels," *Journal of Peace Research*, Vol.28, no.4, 1991, pp. 382–383.

9   Homa Katouzian, *Mussadiq and the Struggle for Power in Iran*, I.B.Tauris, London 1990, p. 48.

10   Ansari, *Modern Iran*, p. 121.

11   Ibid, p. 135.

12   Katouzian, *Mussadiq and the Struggle for Power in Iran*, pp. 151, 155.

13   Ansari, *Modern Iran*, p. 174.

14   Gheissari and Nasr, *Democracy in Iran*, pp. 56–57.

15   April R. Summitt, "For a White Revolution: John F. Kennedy and the Shah of Iran," *Middle East Journal*, Vol.58, no.4, Autumn 2004, p. 564.

16   Vanessa Martin, *Creating an Islamic State: Khomeini and the Making of a New Iran*, I.B.Tauris, London 2000. pp. 62–63.

17   R. Khomeini, "The Granting of Capitulatory Rights to the US," October 27, 1964, in Algar, H. (trans.) *Islam and Revolution: Writings and Declarations of Imam Khomeini*, Berkeley, Mizan Press, 1981, pp. 181–188.

DOI: 10.1057/9781137330178

2

Iranian Encounters with Democracy

Abstract: *Throughout her history, Iran's experiences with the West have been rather paradoxical. While on one hand these experiences have been troubled by violence and exploitation, Western ideas have also acted as an impetus for democratic reform. The second half of the 19th century saw a number of intellectuals advocate judicial, political and economic reforms based on Enlightenment principles, and particularly republicanism, which laid the groundwork for constitutional demands in 1906. Secularist intellectuals were not the only actors responsible for Iranian constitutional transformation, however. The Ulama were crucial in effectively mobilizing the Iranian population around nonviolent resistance strategies such as bast (sanctuary), which were crucial in gaining democratic concessions from the Qajar government.*

Jahanbegloo, Ramin. *Democracy in Iran.* Basingstoke: Palgrave Macmillan, 2013. DOI: 10.1057/9781137330178.

For the past 150 years Iranian elites have been engaged with modern ideas. This engagement has not only been intellectual and cultural but also social and political. It has been at the foundation of two influential events in Iran's history in the 20th century, namely the Iranian Constitutional Revolution of 1906 and the Iranian Revolution of 1979. Scholars of modern and contemporary Iran are often struck by the redundancy and repetition of peculiar features that have shaped Iranian history in a period of 150 years. Many of them agree that European ideas have played an important role in the making of the modern Iranian intellectual sphere and the desire for democracy and change in Iranian society. This influence has been accompanied by many sufferings, challenges and uncertainties, as the two Iranian revolutions of the 20th century exemplify. It goes without saying that the Iranian encounters with the West, either in forms of ideas or power relations, had a great impact on the social, political and economic structures of Iranian society between the mid-19th century and the present. However, it would be insufficient to overview the nature of changes in the Iranian social and political texture without taking into consideration the continuity between traditional and modern Iran and the role exercised by the Shi'ite Ulama in supporting or containing government policies and political movements.

Iran has been witness to numerous Ulama interventions in the past and the present: the demand for the repeal of the Reuter concession in 1873, the struggle for the repeal of the British tobacco monopoly concession in 1891–1892, the Ulama leadership in the Constitutional Revolution of 1906–1911, the Oil Nationalization movement in the early 1950s, the Khomeini movement of 1962 and finally the Revolution of 1979. These movements shared the common purpose of reducing the power of the monarchy and consolidating the social and political foundations of the clerical institutions. Motivated primarily by social and economic interests, the Ulama were able to effectively mobilize the Iranian population and dominate the public sphere and, therefore, play a decisive role in the political processes of Iran in the 19th and 20th centuries. Though a significant portion of the Ulama, like Bouroujerdi and Haeri, retained their quietist tradition, others like Nuri, Modaress, Kashani and Khomeini were politically motivated and socially well-suited to take part in social and political activities all through the 20th century. A good piece of evidence for the influential character of the Ulama's political and social activities is the role played by the Iranian clergy in the weakening of the Iranian state during the Qajar and Pahlavi regimes. On the one hand, the

DOI: 10.1057/9781137330178

impotence of these states to centralize the instruments of power contributed to the legitimacy of the Ulama and their rise to power. On the other
hand, the Ulama's power and their monopoly of traditional thinking
caused the continued weakness of numerous governments in Iran.

Although the making of the two Revolutions in Iran involved a short
and fragile alliance between secular intellectuals and some of the Ulama,
the degree to which these two revolutions were dominated by the
Iranian clergy is a matter of debate. Most of the mainstream historians
of the Iranian Constitutional Revolution and the Iranian Revolution
of 1979 agree to say that in both events the leadership was in the hands
of the Ulama, but some like Fereydoun Adamiyat (in the case of the
Constitutional Revolution) explain the movement for change primarily
in terms of the role played by the secularist intellectuals who had developed ideas of progress, equality, constitutionalism and reform through
their encounters with modernity. Adamiyat views the involvement
of the intellectuals as a significant element because unlike the Ulama,
who wanted to establish theological rule, Iranian intellectuals believed
in rational politics and in the ideas inspired by the "Great French
Revolution."[1]

The intellectual background for such a contribution was laid down in
the 19th century writings of Iranian intellectuals that challenged absolutism and arbitrary political power. It was in relation with this theme
that the idea of parliamentary liberalism was formulated. A shared
conception of law among the leading intellectuals of this period was
the direct outcome of the readings of European thinkers and writers,
which included Francis Bacon, Descartes, Spinoza, Voltaire, Rousseau,
Bentham, Hume and John Stuart Mill. As such, contacts with Western
ideas helped to create a fertile ground for intellectual changes and later
political reforms in Iran. In the late 19th century a number of Iranian
intellectuals living inside and outside Iran became advocates of political
liberalization and social equality. Among them were the playwright Mirza
Fath Ali Akhundzadeh (1812–1878), the writer Abd-al Rahim Talebov
(1834–1911), the socialist thinker Mirza Aqa Khan Kirmani (1854–1896)
and the modernist Mirza Malkum Khan (1834–1908). The latter is most
often credited for his nationalistic views and for his call on the struggle
against government autocracy and increasing domination of Iran by
imperial powers. After Naser al-Din Shah banned Malkum's Freemason
society (the *Faramushkhaneh*) and sent him to exile, Malkum began to
publish a liberal journal by the name of *Qanun* (Law) from London. In

DOI: 10.1057/9781137330178

his widely circulated and read editorials, Malkum denounced openly the lawlessness and tyranny of the Qajars and demanded a popularly elected assembly. As Hamid Algar argues in his book on Malkum Khan, "This call for parliamentary government was a new element in Malkum's political pronouncements. Earlier, in his treatises, he had proposed only the establishment of law and had even defined Iran, in a kind of draft constitution, as 'an absolute monarchy operating through law.' But his disgrace and dismissal, coming at a time of growing discontent and rebellious in Iran, caused him to address himself to a wider audience with more radical proposals."[2] Malkum was not among those Iranian intellectuals who rejected religion in general. However, "his view of Islam suggests that he did not grasp the implications of its fundamental role in Persian society, nor its inherent tension with modernity. Instead, he saw Islam simply as instrumental in bringing about a program of political action."[3]

Unlike Malkum Khan, many other secular intellectuals of the late Qajar period dissociated religion and politics. Akhundzadeh is the most significant representative of the Iranian secular Aufklarers. Despite being Turcophone, Akhundzadeh identified deeply with Iranian nationalism. In his *Maktubat*, Akhundzadeh promoted free thinking and freedom from religious terror and he strongly invited Iranians to liberate themselves from despotism. However, this could only be "achieved via knowledge and knowledge could not be acquired unless through progress, and progress could not be achieved unless by being liberal, and being liberal is not possible without getting rid of [religious] beliefs."[4] For Akhundzadeh, religion in general and Islam in particular were obstacles to social and intellectual progress. That is the reason why he considered a free thinker as somebody who "is not subject to religious terror, and does not believe in what is beyond reason and outside the law of nature."[5] There is no doubt that Akhundzadeh was a reader of John Stuart Mill and David Hume. His purported "Letter from David Hume to the Muslim Clergy of India" written in 1860 and his commentary of Mill's *On Liberty* provide strong evidence for this argument. But one can conclude by reading Akhundzadeh's writings that he "did not share Hume's skepticism and was instead a firm adherent of nineteenth-century positivism."[6] An examination of Akhundzadeh's life and writings suggests that he was an outspoken advocate of secularism and tried to curb clerical power in Iran whenever he found an opportunity. The obsession with religion and with liberal values remained a salient character of Iranian intelligentsia at the end of the 19th century.

DOI: 10.1057/9781137330178

Two of the most influential advocates of judicial and economic modernization in 19th-century Iran were Mirza Yusef Khan Mostashar od-Dowleh and Mirza Huseyn Khan Mushir od-Dowleh. These two men, in the same manner as Kirmani, Malkum Khan and Akhundzadeh, laid some of the groundwork for the Constitutional Revolution of 1906, in the decade of the 1870s. Mushir od-Dowleh was the reformist states-man of his day who was deeply influenced by the Tanzimat reforms. His experiences in Istanbul as a Qajar ambassador to the Ottoman Empire awakened him to the need of applying modern solutions to Iran's social and economic problems. What grieved Mirza Huseyn Khan more than anything else was that the Iranian ruling class and the king himself were so alien to the idea of a parliamentary government. In a dispatch to the Iranian Foreign Ministry he expressed his distress: "I am grieved and know that I am seeking the impossible. I know that what I wish for my country cannot be achieved overnight, and must be attained gradually. But the reason for my sadness is that not only have we made no effort in this direction yet, but that we do not even believe there is anything wrong with our state, or that our affairs need improvement. To the contrary, we believe that we have reached the highest degree of progress, and there is nothing we have to do or to worry about."[7] Mirza Huseyn Khan never took the risk of openly challenging the Iranian Ulama and that was the basic reason for his failure to accomplish his reforms during his own lifetime. His efforts, however, did create a new dynamic within Iran's political and judicial institutions. His strong belief in the advancement of European civilization was translated in a wide range of innovations, from installing gaslights in Tehran to encouraging the Iranian aristocracy to pay more attention to the new methods of education. Mirza Huseyn Khan's reforms did not have an immediate impact on his contemporar-ies; but considering the considerable lack of resources for the reforms and the inadequate executive authority to enforce them, it is a miracle that Mushir od-Dowleh's principles came later to be considered as the standards of modernization in Iran.

While Mushir od-Dowleh was trying to develop and sustain a coher-ent theory of judicial and political reforms, Mirza Yusef Khan Mostashar od-Dowleh, whose major work *Yek Kalameh* (One Word) played an important role in the process of constitutionalism in Iran, was challeng-ing the political backwardness and economic stagnation of Qajar Iran by acknowledging the major achievements of the West. In response to the question, "what was the secret of Europe's progress?" the author reminded

DOI: 10.1057/9781137330178

his readers that the answer was only one word (*yek kalameh*): a state of law. According to Mostashar od-Dowleh the Muslim thinkers "had failed to understand that the basis of Europe's power was not its technological and scientific achievements, but its political and administrative organization as well as its judicial machinery."[8] As a French-speaking Iranian diplomat influenced by the ideals of the French Revolution Mostashar od-Dowleh envisioned a constitutional Iranian state with laws modeled on those of France helping to create new institutions and social forms. The comparison between the Islamic law and the French law led him to talk about the logical, popular and immanent nature of the French law (*loi*) as a basis for the establishment of a constitutional form of government. He did not, however, talk about secularism as a required element for the modernization of Iranian society. Indeed, it may very well be argued that Mirza Yusef was more critical toward the Iranian officials and leaders rather than toward the Iranian Ulama. He truly believed that the Qajar aristocracy had failed to modernize Iran and that as long as Iran did not overcome backwardness and stagnation by adopting the European model, it was in danger of being dominated by European powers. Ultimately, modernization did not come about as Mostashar od-Dowleh had envisioned it in *Yek Kalameh*, but "his strategy of presenting European ideas under the mask of Islam left a profound impact on some educated and religious minded Iranians who played an important role in the constitutional revolution of 1906. These Iranians were converted to the cause of constitutionalism after reading *Yek Kalameh,* which reassured them that borrowing from Europe did not necessarily mean the loss of their religious and cultural identity."[9] However, Mirza Yusef Khan's failure to acknowledge the fundamental discrepancies between European and Islamic traditions did play a delaying role in the making of the secular mind in Iranian intellectual history.

Secularism is usually regarded as a positive achievement of Western civilization. The separation of church and state, the rule of law, enhanced state authority, an independent civil society, the relegation of religious belief to the private sphere, and toleration of religious sects are discussed as immediate consequences of the secular thought in the West. But whereas secularism in the West was and is philosophically and intellectually accompanied with debates on the making of democratic values, in Iran it has been associated with dictatorship, the abrogation of civil liberties and the weakening of the civil society. As one could expect, the Iranian religious community, before and after the

DOI: 10.1057/9781137330178

Constitutional Revolution of 1906–1911, did not welcome the introduction of Westernizing policies in Iran. It is true that the accommodation of modernity in Iran has been associated among intellectuals and the technocratic elite with the gradual development of rationality and a hundred years later with the emergence of a civil society. But it goes without saying that the resistance to modernized politics based on individual autonomy became the prevailing political discourse among the Iranian clergy, technocrats and militaries who were convinced that any modernization from below would be a cause of political chaos.

The Constitutional Revolution of 1906–1911 stands out of the troubled history of modern and contemporary Iran as a significant rupture with the traditional system of government in Persia where in the words of Thomas Herbert, who travelled to Iran in the early years of the 17th century, the king "Have power of life and death; condemn without hearing; dispose of men's persons and estates and as they please without any respect of right; especially at men's death, where there is any considerable estate."[10] The Revolution of 1906, therefore, matters for introducing the republican idea of government in which the Iranian people presented itself as the sole sovereign. In addition to these two points, the Constitutional Revolution of 1906 played an important role in promoting the idea of a nonviolent mass action in Iran. Although masses have been an important catalyst throughout the Iranian history in expressing religious or political dissatisfactions or simply as an instrument of persuasion and coercion in the hands of power builders, it goes without saying that the action of the crowd in the events of the Revolution of 1906 in Iran was predominantly republican in gesture and nonviolent in nature. The Iranian-American historian, Ervand Abrahamian, in his illuminating research on "The Crowd in the Persian Revolution"[11] presents the Iranian demonstrators as "both nonviolent and remarkably rational."[12] According to him, "The vast majority of participants in rallies, demonstrations, and even riots were not criminals, hired thugs, and social riff-raff, but sober and even 'respectable' members of the community. They were merchants, religious authorities, shopkeepers, workshop owners, craftsmen, apprentices, journeymen, and students. The centers of revolutionary crowds were the bazaar and the middle class precincts, not the slums."[13] As such, the one safe generalization that can be sustained is that the Constitutional Revolution of 1906 was a multiclass, popular movement. This dynamic points to the importance of grasping the spontaneous and nonviolent pulse of this event which

DOI: 10.1057/9781137330178

unlike the French Revolution of 1789 and the Russian Revolution of 1917 was not exclusively controlled and dominated by the ideological projects of the political elite like Robespierre and Lenin. According to Ahmad Kasravi, a famous Iranian historian of the Constitutional Revolution, "In Tabriz during the Constitutional Revolution, as in Paris during the French Revolution, the sans-culottes and the property less poor reared their heads. The driving force of these men was toward anarchy. First to overthrow the despotic power of the court, and then to turn against the rich and the propertied classes. It was with the backing of such men that Danton and Robespierre rose to power. In Tabriz no Dantons and Robespierres appeared, but if they had we would also have had a 'reign of terror' "[14]

Despite the absence of charismatic political leaders in the Iranian revolution of 1906–1911 no serious historian or political analyst could underestimate the key role played by the association of guilds in Tehran bazaar. Iran's pattern of urban revolt in the Constitutional Revolution thus partly bears out the resource mobilization views of Charles Tilly that rebels must possess a certain collective organization in order to revolt against the system. Tilly would affirm that "solidarity, rather than insufficient integration, provides the necessary conditions of collective action, and ... rebellions, protest, collective violence, and related forms of action result from rational pursuit of shared interests."[15] Tilly and other resource mobilization theorists commonly assert that solidarity refers to strong social networks. It so happened that in the case of Iranian Constitutional Revolution the absence of a strong state bureaucracy left the streets of Tehran and Tabriz in the hands of the bazaar community and the Shi'ite Ulama who could stand up as rivals to the Qajar political establishment. As Abrahamian affirms, "The first crowd of the Constitutional Revolution took the form of an orderly procession of money-lenders and cloth-merchants delivering a letter of protest to the government."[16] The protest was decided against the Qajar trade policies favoring Russian traders against the interests of the bazaaris. This incident was followed several months later by the bastinadoing of two prominent merchants by the order of the Governor of Tehran. In support of the victims the bazaaris closed their shops and took refuge in a mosque nearby. They were joined by well-known religious leaders like Seyyed Abdullah Behbahani and Seyyed Mohamad Tabatabai. In the following days, seven of the leading religious figures and a handful of students and merchants took of sanctuary in Shah Abd-ol Azim shrine

DOI: 10.1057/9781137330178

near Tehran and demanded from the Shah the formation of a "House of Justice" and the dismissal of the Governor of Tehran.

As we can see clearly from the line-up of social forces in the making of the constitutional alliance those who were involved were mostly urban actors who had specific social and economic grievances against the Qajar state and its foreign partners. Matters came to a point of no return in the summer of 1906 when a large crowd of 14,000 people sought sanctuary (*bast*) in the grounds of the British Legation. Faced with the disciplined, determined and nonviolent action of the urban alliance of merchants, Ulama and the intelligentsia, the Qajar monarch, Mozaffar al-Din Shah, backed down. The *bast* strategy was described in a detailed memorandum by the British Legation to the Foreign Office in London. In this document, the British Legation refers to the *bast* as "an immemorial custom."[17] It would be more correct to refer to the strategy of *bast* as a nonviolent model of resistance against oppression and tyranny. The *bast* model represents a method for increasing the sense of cohesiveness and solidarity in a community through the active promotion of a nonviolent environment. As such, not only does it increase the degree of social immunity of the community to the spread of violence, but it also develops the capacity of democratic learning among the civic actors. If the *bast* strategy could be regarded as a successful nonviolent technique of action in the Iranian Constitutional Revolution, it is mainly due to its orderly adherence to a nonviolent behavior against Qajar opponents who had a total monopoly on political violence. The main characteristic of *bast* as a nonviolent method of social and political struggle is that it took away the legitimacy of the Qajar government forcing it to negotiate with the Iranian civic actors on their demand for the creation of a constituent assembly. Though the Qajar government had previously shown its impressive power in striking religious and social actors of the Iranian society like those belonging to the Babi movement, its internal weaknesses and the surprising disciplined and nonviolent move of the Iranian population forced the Shah to accept the idea of the new constitution. The nonviolent victory of the Iranian crowd in 1906 points to the social awareness and political maturity of different civic actors within a political framework that asserted its legitimacy though social and political forms of violence. As such, the Constitutional Revolution marked the true beginning of the practice of nonviolent techniques in Iranian public sphere. Although principled nonviolence found its cultural roots deep in the Persian pre-Islamic and post-Islamic religious and philosophical

DOI: 10.1057/9781137330178

texts, it was never practiced before in modern Iran in the context of a republican struggle for justice. Therefore, it is not too much to say that without the moral capital of the nonviolent struggle of Iranian urban actors the short-lived revolutionary movement would have paled into a violent and undisciplined protest . As such, nonviolence did much to keep the spirit of constitutionalism alive in Iran.

Notes

1   Fereydoun Adamiyat, *Fekr-e Demokrasi-ye Ejtema'i dar Nehzat-e Mashrutiyat-e Iran* [*The Idea of Social Democracy in the Iranian Constitutional Movement*], Tehran, 1976, p. 3.
2   Hamid Algar, *Mirza Malkum Khan: A Study in the History of Iranian Modernism*, London: University of California Press, 1973, p. 237.
3   Ali Gheissari, *Iranian Intellectuals in the 20th Century*, Austin: University of Texas Press, 1998, p. 27.
4   Mirza Fath Ali Akhundzadeh, *Maktubat*, ed. M. Subhdam, Paris, 1985, p. 56.
5   Ibid., p. 12.
6   Cyrus Masroori, "European Thought in Nineteenth-Century Iran: David Hume and Others," *Journal of the History of Ideas*, Vol. 61, no. 4 (October 2000): 668.
7   26 April 1867, Archives, Ministry of Foreign Affairs, Tehran, Iran, cited in Guit Nashat, *The Origins of Modern Reform in Iran*, 1870–1880, Chicago: University of Illinois Press, 1982, pp. 35–36.
8   Mehrdad Kia, "Constitutionalism, Economic Modernization and Islam in the Writings of Mirza Yusef Khan Mostashar od-Dowleh," *Middle Eastern Studies* Vol. 30, no. 4 (October 1994): 758.
9   Ibid., p. 773.
10 Thomas Herbert, *Travels in Persia, 1617–1629*, new ed., London, 1928, p. 227.
11 Ervand Abrahamian, "The Crowd in the Persian Revolution," *Iranian Studies*, Vol.2, no.4 (Autumn 1969), pp. 128–150.
12 Ibid, p. 146.
13 Ibid.
14 A. Kasravi, *Tarikh-I Mashrtah-I Iran* (*The History of the Persian Constitution*), Tehran 1961, quoted in Abrahamian, Ervand, "The Crowd in the Persian Revolution," p. 141.
15 Tilly Charles, *Big Structures, Large Processes, Huge Comparisons*, New York: Russell Sage Found, 1984, pp. 51–52.
16 Abrahamian, "The Crowd in the Persian Revolution," p. 131.
17 Quoted in Abrahamian, "The Crowd in the Persian Revolution," p. 133.

DOI: 10.1057/9781137330178

3

Democracy and Lawfulness in the Iranian Constitutional Revolution

Abstract: *At the turn of the 20th century, a multiplicity of strong interests emerged within Iran surrounding the nation's course of development, some of which continue to surface in one form or another to this day. Around the time of the Constitutional Revolution these interest were represented by: (a) the Qajar elite, which wished to solidify its control over Iran, (b) intellectuals who demanded Western-style reforms, (c) merchants and bazaaris demanding more economic protection against Western expansion, and (d) the Ulama, whose traditional authority was challenged by a growing state. Although the Ulama was instrumental in the revolutionary struggles of 1906 and 1979, it was their different aims and strategies that led to their defeat in 1906 and triumph in 1979.*

Jahanbegloo, Ramin. *Democracy in Iran*. Basingstoke: Palgrave Macmillan, 2013. DOI: 10.1057/9781137330178.

Nonviolent movements have had a long and strenuous history in 20th-century Iran. As a result of these movements Iran has faced complex and consistent social change, causing two revolutions within the last 100 years. These social changes have come about during various peaks of dissent and protest, when one political discourse has challenged another, and has either failed or succeeded in redirecting Iran's destiny. One such peak was the Constitutional Revolution of 1906–1911. The Constitutional Revolution of 1906–1911 put an end to the rule of the Qajar dynasty, but it also put into question the idea of tyranny. Iranians began to question their government's ability to represent and protect the nation. Strong interests emerged in the struggle to redirect Iran's development in the modern era: those of the Qajar court, who wished to solidify control over Iran; of intellectuals, instilled with the new ideas of Enlightenment Europe; of merchants and bazaaris, threatened by the penetration of Western economic forces; of the Ulama, whose traditional spheres of influence and control were being brought into question by the expanding influence of the state.

It was in this volatile arena that the Constitutional Revolution emerged, bringing about modern conceptions of the rule of law and equality to the Iranian people. The establishment of Iran's first constitution and parliament grew out of a vision that sought to reinstate an era of deep-seated change in Iranian society. The agents of this changed hoped for a new political framework that would disassociate the Iranian nation from its archaic ways of violence and effectively push Iran into the rule of law. The setting with which this move against violence and for the rule of law emerged was certainly a difficult time for the Iranian people. At the turn of the 20th century the country was still coping with the effects of the Qajar kings' lavish lifestyles and a significant abuse of power which was exemplified by the killing of members of the Babi sect. Further resentment was fuelled by the Shah's granting of concessions to Russia and England in order to manage the country's national debt, which gave these European powers significant influence over Iran's economic and political spheres. In retrospect, the mass opposition toward Qajar authority was not unjustified considering the great inconsistency and fraud of the Iranian government, as well as a lack of genuine political infrastructure. According to some historiographers, the composition of the Qajar state in early 1900s closely resembled the Tudor period than any modern ruling system.[1] The various levels of the regime served to implement the Shah's will, and the people were forced to surrender to his

DOI: 10.1057/9781137330178

indisputable power. Furthermore, the political structures at the time prevented a rise in authority to anyone who was not from privileged birth, thus disenfranchising the majority. Iranians were essentially a politically deprived people who had not yet enjoyed the advantages of modern rule of law and liberal values. As such, the public dissatisfaction that emerged in Iran during this period revealed itself in various nonviolent forms, most notably through petitions and strikes.

But perhaps the most notable opposition came with the *bast* movement in 1906. The period of the Constitutional Revolution of 1905–1911 is when the most famous *bast*s were taken. A traditional form of nonviolent protest, *bast* was a form strategy for Iranian citizens to gather at religious shrines, and later at the foreign legations, and claim sanctuary. In 1905, the governor of Tehran ordered that some sugar merchants be bastinadoed for refusing to lower their prices. A group of merchants, tradesmen and mullahs took sanctuary (*bast*) in a Tehran mosque. The beating of several merchants by government officials escalated into new strikes that soon adjourned to a shrine near Tehran, which the demonstrators claimed as a sanctuary. While under sanctuary, the government was unable to arrest or otherwise molest the demonstrators, and a series of such sanctuary protests over subsequent months, combined with wide-scale general strikes of craftsmen and merchants, forced the ailing Shah to grant a constitution in 1906. *Bast* is an old civic gesture in Iranian political culture and a strategy of civil disobedience, which presumably should protect the asylum seekers from violence. This strategy paved the way for active participation of Iranian population in a movement toward the establishment of an Iranian constitution. The *bast* movement as a nonviolent strategy of disobedience did not start as a deliberate move toward constitutionalism in the country, but adopted this goal as a result of the political circumstances. Lambton notes that the Iranian dissidents initially demanded reform, and revolution was not in fact a part of their agenda. Rather, what was desired, as it has usually been the case in contemporary Iranian political history, was a freedom from tyranny and oppression, which is in accordance with the Shi'ite vision of "enjoining that which is good and forbidding that which is evil."[2] The Iranian Constitutional Revolution was a unique political experience in bringing together social actors from different social backgrounds and ideological convictions. Enlightened intelligentsia, members of the powerful Ulama as well as the bazaaris and merchants all came together to further the cause of constitutionalism. For many, however, the Iranian

DOI: 10.1057/9781137330178

Constitutional Revolution had wider ramifications affecting the perception of the present and future conditions of the Iranian people.

The Constitutional Revolution of 1906, which was perhaps the first nonviolent movement of its kind in the Middle East, marked the beginning of the demand for individual rights and the rule of law in Iran. Moreover, the ideas of accountability and reform, as consequences of nonviolent change, entered the Iranian body politic and continued to have a substantial influence on the country's political development for over a century. The nonviolent challenge to the monarchical absolutism of the Qajar dynasty was not only rooted in the work of those merchants and Ulama that favored constitutionalism, but was also developed by the multiple efforts of Iranian intellectuals who paved the road for the modern idea of individual rights in Iran. The Iranian historian Fereydoun Adamiyat considers Iranian intellectuals in late Qajar period as the main animators of the idea of constitutionalism.[3] However, though the ideals of constitutionalism and rule of law were developed by thinkers such as Mirza Malkum Khan, Mirza Aqa Khan Kermani and many others, it was principally through the nonviolent constitutional movement itself that these concepts gained popularity and were tested in Iranian society. As such, the constitutionalist Ulama played the role of mediators who connected the intellectual dissent to a nonviolent movement. This is because, in addition to the socioeconomic and political factors listed above, the Ulama had religious tradition on their side. As John Foran notes, during the Constitutional Revolution "religious imagery played a definite role in mobilizing the masses, particularly the themes of martyrdom and revolt."[4] Only the Ulama, not the unorganized, decentralized state apparatus, could provide an institutional system which could facilitate mass mobilization. This semiautonomous nature meant they could act as a bargaining agent between the state and the population they represented, and could mobilize the masses to thwart state attempts to undermine their power through popular protests against foreign powers or economic concessions.[5]

There were also various other important elements that helped solidify the power of the Ulama. First of all, there was a concentration of influential and respected *mujtahids* who resided in Iraq, outside of the control of the Iranian state, from which pronouncements could be made with impunity.[6] Their extensive system of influence also meant that they could suppress any movement which they deemed harmful to their interests, as was amply portrayed by their reaction to the Babi movement.[7] Also,

DOI: 10.1057/9781137330178

because of their location, close to the people they represented, they had a better understanding of the effects of government policy and were more apt at addressing or inflaming concerns than the aloof government.[8] Finally, and perhaps most importantly to the current study, the Ulama had by this time developed strong ties with the bazaar community. This relationship first began when the Afghan Sunni invaders gained control of Iran after the defeat of the Safavids. At this time, many Ulama suffered downward mobility and looked to create relations with the bazaaris to replace the patronage they had previously received from the Shah.[9] These relations led, over the years, to a mutually reinforcing relationship that would prove to be pivotal during the Constitutional Revolution. One of the most important religious tenets which increased the influence of the Ulama was the idea that each believer had to follow the teachings of a living mujtahid. This created a following among the people for particular *mujtahids*, which gave them power and prestige that they could exploit during the Constitutional Revolution.[10] This idea of the interpretation of religious law came from the Usul'i school of jurisprudence. The separation of all Shi'ites into laymen and experts and the belief that all laymen must emulate an expert supported and helped establish the leading role of the Ulama in society.[11] Combined with this was the idea of having one supreme source of emulation, known as the *marja'-e taqlid*. This idea stated that there should be one *marja'-e taqlid* who could issue *fatwas* binding on all believers.[12] This became especially important during the Tobacco Concessions and the Constitutional Revolution, when the *marja'-e taqlid* abandoned their apolitical stance, and served as a rallying figure for the religious community: "The institution of a supreme source for emulation introduced the possibility of a strong, centralized leadership."[13] This also harks back to the messianic ideals mentioned earlier.

These important evolutions in the power of the Ulama did not converge spontaneously during the Constitutional Revolution, but rather were cemented and expanded a decade and a half earlier during the Tobacco Concessions. The Tobacco Concessions provide an interesting study for the emergence of trends of power relations which would become increasingly important as the Constitutional Revolution began to take shape. As Keddie explains, "the movement was the first successful mass protest in modern Iran, combining Ulama, modernists, merchants, and ordinary townspeople in a coordinated move against government policy."[14] Moreover, "the movement had demonstrated how the leading Ulama, from the position of relative impunity, could mobilize both

DOI: 10.1057/9781137330178

the resentment and the religious feelings of the masses in a way that the reformers could never hope to duplicate on their own."[15] It led to an increase in the power of the Ulama, and "it witnessed the birth of a peculiar modern Iranian tradition of mosque-bazaar-intelligentsia alliance against the state."[16] Thus, the Tobacco Concessions were important for three reasons: they cemented and increased the power of the Ulama, showed an ability on their part to mobilize the masses that would be essential to reform movements in the future, and created and solidified an alliance between the Ulama, the bazaaris and the intellectuals, which would prove essential in the Constitutional Revolution.

It is important to keep in mind that the Ulama were not the catalysts to the Constitutional Revolution, but rather were one of many factors (albeit an important one) that built up grievances and eventually led to the popular revolution in 1906. As Keddie notes, "there is nothing intrinsic in Shi'ism to make it revolutionary, and the anti-establishment nature of Iran's clerical leadership at various recent points must be explained mainly by historical change and circumstance."[17] With the outbreak of the Constitutional Revolution, the ability of the Ulama to instigate political action among the masses proved vital to the success of the movement. At some point many, if not most, Ulama supported the revolution. They saw the revolution as a way to further their cause of opposition to the state. This had an enormous impact and shows the extent to which the clergy were fully and inextricably woven into the social fabric, and how much control and influence they had over the people of Iran.[18] The Ulama's "role in enlisting a large part of the urban population in anti-royalist causes...helps explain the frequent mobilization of large sections of the population in rebellious or revolutionary movements."[19] Plus, their participation helped ensure religion retained its important place in Iranian society and government, and the new order did not threaten the social power position of the Ulama.[20]

As much influence and importance as the Ulama and their leading members had, they were still being pushed by the intellectuals to champion the cause of constitutionalism. However, the Ulama often seemed to be involved in the Revolution to forward their own interests rather than champion those of other groups of Iranians. The Ulama largely were concerned with the threat to their traditional sphere of authority, and their involvement in 1906 was mainly an attempt to protect that authority.[21] The alliance was in fact uneasy, which is evidenced by its breakup following the initial revolution; furthermore, the Ulama were

DOI: 10.1057/9781137330178

highly suspicious of the foreign ideas championed by the intellectuals and constitutionalists, and a split emerged between those that favored reform and those that were not keen to see a social or political restructuring.[22] Their interests lay in gaining more local power and reversing the gains of the state in its encroachment on the spheres of life traditionally controlled by the Ulama, such as religious courts and education.[23]

Many historians continue to maintain that the Ulama were an essential factor in the development of the Constitutional Revolution. However, some of them had consistently supported monarchical absolutism and even figures like Sheikh Fazlollah Nuri rejected constitutionalism as a Western idea. For others, such as Mohammad Hossein Naini, constitutionalism was not a threat to Shi'ite Islam, but in fact was an imperative to preserving it. Thus religion was not considered by all the Ulama as an automatic obstacle to a nonviolent strategy of constitutionalism. On the contrary, to the extent that constitutionalism was a demand to reduce the violence of the state in Iran, it was expected to coexist with a nonviolent expression of Shi'ite Islam. In the end, however, this was not a religious revolution. It wasn't secular either, but the major ideological underpinnings were not primarily concerned with maintaining the primacy of religion, and the intellectuals who constructed the theoretical underpinnings of the movement were only concerned with religion in so far as it could be used to spread the revolution and garner support.[24] One may wonder why this was the case. Iran did in fact see a religious revolution a little over 70 years after the beginning of the Constitutional Revolution. Why were the religious elements involved able to coopt the nonviolent and legalist narrative of the Constitutional Revolution while they failed to do it in 1979?

When comparing 1906 to 1979, two major themes emerge which differentiate the success of the religious movement in 1979 and its failure in 1906. First, members of the religious faction in 1906 were deeply divided in their theological and ideological opinions. Second, and intrinsically tied to this, is the fact that in 1906 the religious elites were pushed toward the concepts of constitutionalism and representation. It is true that both revolutions were able to garner a broad coalition of social groups and classes, due to the repressive policies of the Qajar and Pahlavi dynasties and the inclusive nature of the revolutionary objectives. However, the nonviolent origins of the secular–religious alliance that coalesced during the Tobacco Protest in 1891 allowed nonviolent strategies to gain momentum and to advocate for moderation and negotiations in the

DOI: 10.1057/9781137330178

Constitutional Revolution of 1906. The objective of the 1906 Revolution was to limit the power of the Shah and to create a House of Justice (*Edalat Khaneh*), not to establish a new regime. The revolutionaries in 1906 adhered to the ideals of justice and parliamentarianism, which led to their demand for the creation of the *Majlis*, the national representative assembly. Thus, unlike the Revolution of 1979, the raison d'être of the Constitutional Revolution was to ensure the protection of the rights of the individual and to bring order to society, politics and economy.

The reformist and legalist elements of the Constitutional movement would confound the democratic passion of the constitutionalists with the nonviolent strategies of the social actors of the event, a development that would determine the future of nonviolent action in Iranian politics after 1906. But this was not enough to stop the revival of old hostilities: "In pursuing their goals of establishing a constitutional regime and getting rid of despotism, the different groups that were active in the movement ignored the many inherent contradictions in their programs and social plans. Achievement of the immediate goals ended the loose coalition of divergent interests and ideas, and old hostilities were revived."[25] Iranians lost their democracy as quickly as they got it. Democratic consolidation seemed more difficult than democratic inspiration. The Ulama, who felt threatened by the secular nature of the Constitutional movement, made sure that all legislation was in accordance with Islamic law. Meanwhile the Shah, fed up with the demands of the *Majlis* and continued diminishment of his authority, soon enlisted the help of the Russian-led Cossack Brigade to assist him with his overthrow of the *Majlis* in 1907. But despite the return to despotism, the Iranian Constitutional movement was not left without a drive for independence. This resistance took the form of nonviolent protests and public lobbying against the monarch and his military, who could hardly quell the people's defiance. The movement was very much a grassroots effort with local leaders encouraging residents of different cities of Iran like Tabriz, Rasht and Isfahan to ignore the Shah's order for surrender. The resistance grew to the point that royal troops became powerless in disbanding the movement, which had continued to spread throughout the provinces. With the defeat of Muhammad Ali Shah's Lesser Autocracy one of the Constitutional movement's greatest impediments was removed. But it also gravely weakened the image of stability and order in the mind of Iranians.

Nonviolent resistance to tyranny and constructive politics became dissociated from one another and the weakness of central government and

DOI: 10.1057/9781137330178

factional struggle in the *Majlis* encouraged foreign powers to promote the division of Iran. Throughout the Constitutional Revolution, Russian and British forces managed to increase their hold in the country; Russia in the North, England in the South. The overthrow of a Shah sympathetic to these foreign powers seemed to do little to diminish their control of Iran. As the two main powers in the country during this time, Russia and England felt it was their responsibility to select administrative authorities, and any figures chosen by Iranians without their consent might jeopardize their interests. After dispatching an ultimatum to the *Majlis*, several parliamentary deputies refused to submit to imperial demands. They were supported by a huge anti-imperialistic resistance outside the parliament, but despite the widespread demonstrations against foreign powers, parliamentary forces had no choice but to suspend the *Majlis*. All that the Constitutional forces had worked so hard to achieve in a revolution that lasted five years was forcibly destroyed by outside forces. As Morgan Shuster, an administrative expert from America, later described it, "It was a sordid ending to a gallant struggle for liberty and enlightenment."[26] The year 1911 marked the suspension of a significant moment of rightful and nonviolent democratization in Iranian history.

Certainly on a short-term level the defeat of the Constitutional Revolution can be seen as an overall failure of nonviolence and rule of law in Iran. No doubt, the Constitutional Revolution did fall short of establishing firm political grounds for nonviolence in Iran, but all that was accomplished before and after at the level of ideas ultimately served to outweigh its shortcomings in Iranian contemporary history. Many Iranian historians believe that the Constitutional Revolution focused too much on a European model of constitutionalism that was incompatible with the true nature of Iranian society during that period.[27] Others contribute this failure to the dispute between the conservative Ulama and the secular reformers. Nonviolent reform and dialogue were therefore unable to take place without some sort of conformity between the pro-constitutional Ulama and the secular forces. For many then, the Constitutional Revolution was an unfinished project. Its goals of eradicating injustice and inequality were only temporarily realized and in fact the lawful nonviolence that was envisioned by many of the pre-revolutionary elites was never fully attained. Yet despite the absence of any significant social and economic changes, the Constitutional Revolution can be viewed from a political and philosophical perspective as having great magnitude. It demonstrates a milestone in Iranian

DOI: 10.1057/9781137330178

history of nonviolence that would introduce the country to many democratic and nonviolent ideals that were formerly absent. Furthermore, a critique of authority and a discourse on disobedience entered into Iran's consciousness following the Revolution. Since such achievements are a testament to the Constitutional Revolution's ability to influence the history of nonviolence in Iran, it would be unwise to suggest that the circumstances had no effect on the general political mood and behavior of Iranians. Furthermore, despite the short-term failures, the opportunities that the Revolution of 1906 provided for Iran's future are immeasurable. The movement and its ideals of anti-authoritarianism and disobedience would continue in the future uprisings and democratic experiences such as the Mossadeq movement for the nationalization of oil and the Iranian Revolution of 1979. Lastly and most significantly, the Revolution of 1906 continues to be seen by younger generation of Iranians, active today in the Green Movement, as a stepping stone for future progress of nonviolence in Iranian society.

In the past, the political failure of the 1906 Revolution largely discredited its short-term philosophical influences and pushed Iranian elites to search for more violent methods of mobilization. Ervand Abrahamian argues that due to the much more extreme level of repression under the Pahlavi regime, the younger generations of Iranian revolutionaries developed much more radical ideas than their predecessors.[28] During the 1970s many of the Iranian youth turned toward Ayatollah Khomeini's leadership due to their disillusionment with traditional secular leadership. Many who considered that the Iranian elites had failed to halt the westernization of Iran perceived the religious authorities as more protective of the Iranian nation. Hence Ayatollah Khomeini's concept of Islamic governance became a very attractive alternative for a diversity of groups. His anti-imperialist discourse appealed to many of the center-left and radical leftist groups, while his religious rhetoric appealed to the lower rural and urban groups.

In contrast to 1906, the actors of 1979 had a coherent plan and were united in their goal to end with the Pahlavi state under Khomeini's leadership. The importance of this coherence and agreement in 1979 becomes even more apparent when contrasted with the other ideological perspectives. Most importantly, the liberals (and moderates) and the Left did not have a coherent scheme for the realization of their goals after the revolution, similar to the religious factions in 1906.[29] Therefore, they were overrun by the religious forces. Another important distinction was

DOI: 10.1057/9781137330178

the level of credit given to the religious forces. In 1979, the Left thought that the religious forces were politically unsophisticated and irrelevant to the socioeconomic demands of the nation – as such they would not be able to take control.[30] The second major distinction between the religious movement in 1906 and that of 1979 is the lack of a charismatic leader able to unify the movement. In 1906, there were three major religious leaders: Tabataba'i, Behbehan'i and Nuri. There were problems with the leadership of all three. Tabataba'i, "despite his popularity and the sincerity of his motives ... did not have the disposition and interpersonal communication skills necessary for effective leadership."[31] Behbehan'i was mistrusted by many, and was seen as likely to abandon the cause if it suited his needs.[32] Nuri was opposed to the modernization projects forwarded by the revolution and was in direct opposition, after 1906, to the other two leaders; while a very popular *mujtahid* in Iran, he would not and was not able to coopt their power.[33] Thus, the religious movement had no single figure to follow. This is in sharp contrast to the reality of 1979. Ayatollah Khomeini was a charismatic leader who was a figure able to win over the masses. Therefore, even after he "retired" to Qom, he continued to largely control the direction of the revolution and the evolution of the new Islamic state.[34] He was able to use this massive amount of personal character to coopt the other ideologies and groups. He was also able to far outstrip in popularity the leaders of the other movements.

It goes without saying that even though the state did not become governed by Islamic law after the Constitutional Revolution, religion played a vital role in the development of the events leading up to and following 1906. But there were many other factors which came into play and caused the Constitutional Revolution to evolve as it did. The raison d'être of the Constitutional Revolution was to establish the rule of law, not an Islamic government. Ayatollah Khomeini was very careful to use an inclusive rhetoric, so as not to divide the coalition during the Revolution of 1979. But he felt that the only option of the revolutionary movement was to overthrow the Shah, purge Iran from Western influence, and reassert its Islamic character. Ayatollah Khomeini's anti-liberal attitude was supported by many intellectual currents in Iran that had turned their back to the nonviolent constitutionalism of 1906. While Jalal Al-Ahmad was adopting an anti-imperialist view of Shi'ism as a mobilizing political against what he called the "westoxication" of Iran, Ali Shariati was formulating a revolutionary interpretation of Islam as a

DOI: 10.1057/9781137330178

counterweight to Marxism and Liberalism. Shariati argued that to fight imperialism the peoples of the Third World had to reassert their cultural identity. For Iranians, this was perceived as a renewal of the religious layer of Iranian identity. He also argued that Islam should not be perceived as an apolitical force but rather a revolutionary ideal that could inspire Muslims to fight oppression and injustice.[35] Shariati's audience was, however, more among the younger generation of educated Iranians rather than among the religious establishment, because he argued that the traditional Ulama had colluded with the Iranian state, institutionalizing Shi'ism and becoming oppressive. Another influential intellectual figure in the Revolution of 1979 was Mehdi Bazargan, who advocated that there should be no divide between Islam and politics since Islam offers direction on political, economic and social issues.[36] Additionally, Bazargan was an important figure in the National Resistance Movement which advocated for a combination of Mossadeqist nationalism and Shi'ite Islam to bridge the gap between modern nationalists and traditional Islamists in Iran.

Evidently, the intellectual motivations and justifications for the Revolution of 1979 were considerably different from and also more divergent than those that existed in 1906. Therefore, it would be too simplistic to portray 1906 as an inspiration for 1979. It is true, however, that in both revolutions the Ulama played an entrenched role in Iranian society and politics, and were thus very close to the masses. Moreover, in both cases there was a growing disapproval of the West and liberal ideas among traditionalist clerics. According to Sandra Mackey, "the traditionalists within the Ulama, the great majority of the clerics, quaked before the ideas of the West descending on Qajar Iran. Regardless of what it might promise in the way of a national revival, Westernization to the guardians of Shi'ism meant secularization with its attendant rejection of Islam's central role in defining Iran's cultural and political identity."[37] As such, in both revolutions the Ulama had the means to promulgate their agendas in mosques, gatherings and through *fatwas*. In the case of the Constitutional Revolution of 1906, "Only the Ulama could, in theory, provide the institutional backing for opposition to Qajar rule."[38] Thus as in 1979, in the interest of a victory against the monarchy, those who carried the ideas of nonviolence and liberal values abandoned critical rationality in order to win the support of the Ulama.

The concessions to the traditionalist Ulama after the first draft of the constitution in 1906 are the best examples of the decline of the

DOI: 10.1057/9781137330178

Constitutional Revolution and with it the idea of nonviolence. The constitution was originally inclined toward a nonviolent secularism, but this was quickly contested by the conservative Ulama who underlined the rule of Shari'a law against a constitutional law that would contain tyranny and political violence. Hence, Sheikh Fazlollah Nuri came to the forefront of clerical opposition, denouncing a man-made constitution as a blueprint against the will of God: "While Nuri pressed his virulent attack on the constitution as a Western document, the constitutionalists within the *Majlis* loaded shell after shell into his cannon. From early 1907, the secular constitutionalists unabashedly copied Europe. When they wrote the constitution for Iran, they all but duplicated the 1831 Belgian constitution."[39] This duplication, however, was only part of the problem, and this was only the beginning of the struggle between nonviolent constitutionalism and violent traditionalism in Iranian contemporary history. The anti-constitutional spirit which grew in intensity with Nuri's frequent condemnations and increasing support of the Shari'a law was underlined systematically and authoritatively 70 years later by Ayatollah Khomeini in his doctrine of *velayat-e-faqih*.

The inclusion of the concept of *velayat-e-faqih* signified the institutionalization of theocratic violence in Iran under the authority of the Iranian clergy. The eschatological resonance of this theologico-political decision was not only the process of waiting for the return of the hidden Imam as a future-oriented utopia or the return to an idealized Islamic past, but also total control on every aspect of the individual's life including economic and political matters, as well as the attitudes, values and beliefs of the Iranian population. As a result, there were no autonomous associations, nor any recognized private/public distinction. That is to say, the Iranian revolution of 1979 and its aftermath involved a rapid transformation of Iranian society and its values according to a new ideological framework. Apart from its ideological and religious structures the Iranian regime had one name, one identity and one essence: violence. Violence became the real and dominant political value for the Islamic regime and with time it turned into an integrated system and became a social culture. The real world of Iranians turned into an absurd and utterly monstrous reality. The objective was to pervert Iranian subjects into a mass of fragmented individuals, to suppress their common world and substitute it with alienation from oneself, from each other and from the outside world. Life was attacked in the very noble aspects that usually guarantee it.

DOI: 10.1057/9781137330178

Eventually, the unreality of horror created its own counter-reality. In such a world, the question of survival was not simply a biological matter, but that of creating one's own identity by achieving an internal mode of thinking. A variety of individual identities – ranging from artists who practiced their art regardless of how it was censored and banned by the official institutions, to intellectuals who privately taught young people outside the sphere of universities controlled by the Iranian state and pluralist Muslims who carried on a resistance to the theocratic system – tried to re-establish their human dignity in the face of terror and humiliation. Their battle was against cowardice and lies, it was based on the refusal to sanction evil. They all shared a common concern with the defense of the private realm of individuality and the creation of a public sphere allowing individuation. This common concern has been of no small import in the resistance to Iranian theocracy and the rise of nonviolence in Iranian public sphere. Today, more than 30 years later, the continuous nonviolent resistance of civil society in Iran suggests the possibility of a more active conjunction between personal individuation and democratic individuation, a relation which recognizes both the distinctive character of a nonviolent temperament and the necessary concerns of all Iranian citizens with a re-vitalized public sphere. Without a doubt, the political and moral enslavement of Iranian citizens has come to its end, not because the regime has put an end to its politics of fear and violent threats on individuals, but because the spirit and the moral foundation that give rise to a refusal of fear and violence and institution of nonviolence are already present. In Ibsen's *The Pillars of Society,* written in 1877, we find a sentence in tune with Iran and its battle with violence: "A moment may come, a word may be spoken, and you and all your splendor will collapse."[40] This has laid out a clear picture for the possibility of nonviolent change in Iran. But before delving further into the need for practical nonviolence in the Iranian public sphere, one needs to turn back to other reasons for its past failure, the most pertinent experience being the fall of Mossadeq and Iranian liberalism in the 20th century.

Notes

1   Haleh Afshar, *Iran: A Revolution in Turmoil*, London: Macmillan Press, 1985, p.122.

2   A.K.S. Lambton, *Qajar Persia: Eleven Studies*, London: I.B.Tauris, 1987, p.322.

DOI: 10.1057/9781137330178

3 Fereydoun Adamiyat, *Fekr-e Azadi va Moqaddameh-ye Nehzat-e Mashroutiyat-e Iran* [*The Idea of Liberty and the Beginning of the Iranian Constitutional Movement*] (Tehran, 1961–1962).

4 John Foran, "The Strengths and Weaknesses of Iran's Populist Alliance: A Class Analysis of the Constitutional Revolution of 1905–1911," *Theory and Society* 20.6 (December 1991): 806.

5 Azar Tabari, "The Role of the Clergy in Modern Iranian Politics," *Religion and Politics in Iran: Shiism from Quietism to Revolution*, New Haven: Yale University Press, 1983, p.49.

6 Juan Cole and Nikki R. Keddie, (eds) *Shi'ism and Social Protest*, New Haven and London: Yale University Press, 1986, p.10.

7 Mangol Bayat, *Iran's First Revolution: Shi'ism and the Constitutional Revolution of 1905–1909*, Oxford: Oxford University Press, 1991, p.33.

8 Peter Avery, *Modern Iran*, New York: Frederick A Praeger Publishers, 1965, p.95.

9 Cole and Keddie, *Shi'ism and Social Protest*, p.9.

10 Nikki Keddie, *Religion and Politics in Iran*, New Haven: Yale University Press, 1983, p.6.

11 Juan Cole, "Imami Jurisprudence and the Role of the Ulama," ed. Nikki Keddie, *Religion and Politics in Iran*, New Haven: Yale University Press, 1983, p.33.

12 Keddie, *Religion and Politics in Iran*, p.9.

13 Cole, "Imami Jurisprudence and the Role of the Ulama," p.34.

14 Nikki Keddie, *Modern Iran: Roots and Results of Revolution*, New Haven: Yale University Press, 2006, p.62.

15 Bayat, *Iran's First Revolution*, p.18.

16 Ibid., p.31.

17 Nikki Keddie, *Iran and the Muslim World: Resistance and Revolution*, New York: New York University Press, 1995, p.176.

18 Ervand Abrahamian, "The Causes of the Constitutional Revolution in Iran," *International Journal of Middle East Studies* 10.3, (August 1979): 403–407.

19 Keddie, *Iran and the Muslim World*, p.65.

20 Ali Gheissari and Vali Nasr, *Democracy in Iran: History and Quest for Liberty*, New York: Oxford University Press, 2006, pp.30–32.

21 Bayat, *Iran's First Revolution*, p.21.

22 Tabari, "The Role of the Clergy in Modern Iranian Politics," p.57.

23 Willen N. Floor, "The Revolutionary Character of the Ulama: Wishful Thinking or Reality?" in Nikki Keddie, *Religion and Politics in Iran*, New Haven: Yale University Press, 1983, p.75.

24 Janet Afary, *The Iranian Constitutional Revolution, 1906–1911: Grassroots Democracy, Social Democracy and the Origins of Feminism*, New York: Columbia University Press, 1996, p.43.

DOI: 10.1057/9781137330178

25 Majid Mohammadi, *Judicial Reform and Reorganization in 20th Century Iran: State-Building, Modernization and Islamicization*, New York: Routledge, 2008, p.60.

26 Quoted in Farhang Holakouee-Naeinee, *The Constitutional Revolution of Iran, 1906: A Sociological Analysis*, Michigan: Xerox University Microfilms, 1974.

27 Ibid., p.157.

28 Ervand Abrahamian, *Iran between Two Revolutions*, Princeton: Princeton University Press, 1983, p.451.

29 Gheissari and Nasr, *Democracy in Iran*, pp.90–95.

30 Ibid., p.93.

31 Bayat, *Iran's First Revolution*, p.123.

32 Afary, *The Iranian Constitutional Revolution*, p.50.

33 Ibid.

34 Ali Ansari, *Modern Iran: The Pahlavis and After*, London: Longman, Pearson Education, 2003, p.221.

35 Abrahamian, *Iran Between Two Revolutions*, pp.465–468.

36 Nikki R. Keddie, *Modern Iran: Roots and Results of Revolution*, New haven, Connecticut, Yale University Press, 2006, pp.198–199.

37 Sandra Mackey, *The Iranians*, New York: Plume, 1988, p.135.

38 Ibid., p.138.

39 Ibid., p.150.

40 Ibsen Henrik, *Pillars of Society*, The Gutenberg Project Ebook, 2007. Accessed January 22, 2013, http://www.gutenberg.org/files/2296/2296.txt.

DOI: 10.1057/9781137330178

4

The Road to Authoritarian Violence: From the Coup of 1953 to the Revolution of 1979

Abstract: *Mossadeq's sympathies towards liberalism and nonviolence, and his advocacy of civic nationalism, provoked powerful domestic and international enemies, which ultimately led to his demise in 1953. Aside from the United States and Britain, powerful domestic actors such as the CIA's principle man General Zahedi, Ayatollah Kashani and the violent fundamentalist group Feda'iyan-e Islam were instrumental in inciting violence that resulted in the coup. Following the coup, the Shah and his political allies placed their faith in ruling through an authoritarian dictatorship. On the eve of the 1979 revolution, two dominant opposition groups stood out. Marxism influenced the first group, while the other marched under the banner of Islamic revivalism. Fatally, both intellectual groups put their faith in Ayatollah Khomeini – unknowingly digging their graves.*

Jahanbegloo, Ramin. *Democracy in Iran*. Basingstoke: Palgrave Macmillan, 2013. DOI: 10.1057/9781137330178.

The overthrow of Prime Minister Mohammad Mossadeq by the intelligence agencies of the United States and Great Britain in August 1953 occupies an immensely significant place in the evolution of intellectual consciousness and discourse in Iran. The coup and its consequences marked a clear rupture with the lawful and nonviolent aspirations of the Iranian elites which were mainly formulated and experienced during the Constitutional Revolution of 1906. Mossadeq's rise to leadership in the movement for the nationalization of the Iranian oil industry and his premiership can be explained as a direct consequence of Iran's encounter with modernity and the nationalist aspirations of Iranian urban middle-class against imperialist intrusions. The close affiliation of Mossadeq with the liberal and nonviolent values of the Revolution of 1906 and his advocacy for a civic nationalism in Iran reinforced his position as the head of a movement that contested foreign imperial hegemony while promoting democratic constitutionalism. As such, the convergence between the evolutions of international politics and Iranian society made it possible for Mossadeq to speak on behalf of the nation, challenging the dominant radical narratives of the Iranian Left and the Islamic groups.

Mossadeq's discourse and action differed markedly from those of Shah's previous prime ministers and clearly the Pahlavi regime had more reason to oppose and undermine actively the democratic spirit of Mossadeq's nonviolent action. It is true that, "Many leading bazaar merchants, as well as several prominent clerics, actively supported Mossadeq," however, "an apathetic, opportunistic, or cynical urban underclass was easy prey for mob leaders and could be manipulated by opponents of Mossadeq."[1] As prime minister, Mossadeq alarmed not only the Shah, by his civic measures of accountability, and the West, through his opposition to the use of the country's oil reserves by the British, but also appeared as a threat to the Tudeh Party and its pro-Soviet policies, through his advocacy of a neutralist stand in his foreign policy, and to the Iranian conservative clerics, because of his commitments to parliamentary procedures and political and civil rights. Therefore, "While the Tudeh Party denounced Mossadeq for his 'fascist' policies in restraining the party, Mossadeq's other opponents, particularly right-wingers and traditionalists blamed him for allowing the party free rein."[2] Despite the fact that Mossadeq received valuable support and collaboration from some high-ranking clerics – some like Sayyed Mahmoud Taleqani, Haj Aqa Reza Zanjani and Shaikh Bah'ai Din Mahallati remained loyal to his cause until the end – leading figures like Ayatollah Kashani began

DOI: 10.1057/9781137330178

to fall out with Mossadeq's Popular Movement and demonstrated clear and active hostility toward it. Actually, Kashani played a more significant role in undermining Mossadeq than those royalists who argued that Mossadeq was overthrown in a national uprising by the Iranian people and a faithful army to the Shah.

It is true that Mossadeq's coalition had become very fragile in 1952, but he still could count on the loyalty of members of the Iranian army and police. The British candidate to overthrow Mossadeq was General Fazlollah Zahedi, though he had been interned by the same British as a pro-Nazi during the Allies occupation of Iran in 1941. "By early 1953 Kashani and the other defectors [of the National Front] had begun to collaborate with Zahedi. The most important such instance of collaboration prior to the coup came in February 1953, when Kashani and Behbehani organized violent demonstrations with disturbances fomented by allies of Zahedi. These events almost toppled Mossadeq and revealed his weaknesses very clearly, presaging the August 19 coup. Kashani also gave Zahedi sanctuary in parliament, enabling him to avoid arrest."[3] Next to the high-rank clerics, the CIA's principal man, General Zahedi and the Tudeh Party, another important contributor to the downfall of Mossadeq and the road to violence in the Iranian society was the Islamic fundamentalist group of Feda'iyan-e Islam, founded by Mojtaba Navvab Safavi.

The Feda'iyan-e Islam became one of the most violent political groups in Iran and mortal enemies of democracy and Mossadeq. From 1945 to 1963, members of this group carried out a series of political assassinations, whose targets included not only government officials but intellectuals such as the prolific Iranian historian and author Ahmad Kasravi and Dr. Hussein Fatemi, Mossadeq's deputy and foreign minister. According to Fakhreddin Azimi, "The Feda'iyan's views were reflected in the demands they made of Mossadeq, which included the imposition of the veil, the expulsion of female employees from government positions, a ban on the sale and consumption of alcoholic beverages, and obligatory public prayer for all government employees. Mossadeq's not unexpected refusal to entertain such demands provided the Feda'iyan with the requisite justification to unleash their hostility against him."[4] Navvab Safavi celebrated the fall of Mossadeq, on August 25, 1953, by publishing a declaration and asking the Shah to follow the precepts of Islam

> If Mossadeq's government had remained [in power] for another two days and the power plays of the foreign worshipers had continued, the anger of the Muslim people would have exploded with more force than it did and

DOI: 10.1057/9781137330178

they would have pulled out with their hands and teeth the veins of everyone of the despicable lackeys of the Soviet Union... This country was saved by Islam and with the power of the faith... The Shah and prime minister have to be believers in, and promoters of, Shi'ism, and the laws that are in opposition to the divine laws of God... must be nullified... The intoxicants, the shameful exposure and carelessness of women, and sexually provocative music... must be done away with and the superior teachings of Islam... must replace them. With the implementation of Islam's superior economic plan, the deprivation of the Muslim people of Iran, and the dangerous class difference would end. [In this way] the Shah and the legitimate government can live in peace and happiness. On this matter our revealing book (the program of the *Feda'iyan-e Islam*) has shown the way.[5]

As we can see, the Shah was rather a small contributor to the mob violence against Mossadeq, and as later in the revolution of 1979, his decisions and actions were partly controlled and manipulated by the US leadership.

The explanation to the success of the coup of 1953 against Mossadeq, however, resides not only in the political weaknesses of Iranian institutions of the day, but can be underlined in relation with Mossadeq's non-violent personality and his refusal to act forcefully against his opponents. In addition to the tactical mistakes that were made by Mossadeq and his National Front colleagues, one needs to point to the role of violent mob as the focus of political movements in Iranian contemporary history. "In the rioting of August 17 the mob was the vortex around which the balance of political forces rotated."[6] The role played by the local gang-leader Shaban Jafari, known as Shaban Beemokh ("Brainless") during the coup of 1953 and later in Mohammad Reza Shah's regime, superbly describes the use of violence to impose social control or to achieve mob rule in contemporary Iran. This mob violence had no decision-making structure and came together for political reasons. But the mob disturbances which persisted in the wake of the coup of 1953 against Mossadeq suggest quite clearly that the coup cannot be blamed solely on Zahedi and the foreign actors, but also on Iranian mob psychology as the principal generator of social hostility and political violence.

There exist many examples of mob psychology in modern and contemporary Iran, the coup d'état of 1953 being just one of them. From the anti-Babi sentiments and pogroms during the Qajar era to the culture of violence promoted by the Islamic republic and perpetuated by staging various forms of physical punishments in public, mob psychology in

DOI: 10.1057/9781137330178

Iran shows that Iranians tend to behave in a different manner as part of a group in contrast to acting independently. As members of thug groups they are likely to commit acts they would never commit alone. This is not due to change in their beliefs or principles, but rather the fact that they tend to ignore or avoid their moral conscience or rational judgment. It is true that the role of mobs in the political evolution of contemporary Iran cannot supply solely a sociological analysis for Iranian society. But what it can reveal is plenty of evidence for a structural violence in Iranian society which has completed the system of arbitrary rule throughout the Iranian history. It goes without saying that in a society as unpredictable as Iran, the mob rule has been and is still largely in the hands of anti-democratic forces which are massively in favor of a political development in the direction of organized violence. According to N. Marbury Efimenco, "Outbursts of protest, as in mob demonstrations, act as cathartic agents in the body politic. Even in its misery the mob reaches a point of futility and exhaustion with its exertions. Particularly in Iran the manifestations of mob action are confined to the cities and rarely penetrate the agricultural hinterland, where the mass of peasantry reside. In a fragmented society the radiation of political forces have no channel of communications to transmit the impulses to the four corners of the nation. Thus, political upheavals quickly spend themselves, and the status quo is soon re-established on the political scene."[7] Efimeco adds: "In the rioting of August 17 (1953) the mob was the vortex around which the balance of political forces rotated."[8]

Thus, Mossadeq's opponents used planned and strategic violence continuously against him and his allies in order to weaken the rule of law and democratic practices. It is therefore difficult to think how Mossadeq's nonviolent premiership would have survived, even if the Americans had not decided to prepare a coup against him. As Homa Katouzian underlines correctly, "Mossadeq and the Popular Movement – whatever their shortcomings... believed in a plural as well constitutional society and did not wish to eliminate anyone else."[9] In addition to this, in the absence of financial assistance provided to the Iranian crowd to buy off their loyalty, it is difficult to imagine how Mossadeq's government would have survived its financial crisis. "Added to the impending bankruptcy were frequent statements of the National Front indicating an indifference toward a Tudeh-led seizure of power. Undoubtedly Washington feared that the strength of the Tudeh party increased in direct proportion to the irresponsibility shown 'ay the National Front. The threat of a possible

DOI: 10.1057/9781137330178

victory of the Tudeh elements endangered American efforts to keep Soviet influence out of the Iranian corridor at the head of the Persian Gulf. A Tudeh-dominated government at Teheran meant the creation of a satellite tied to Moscow and a turning of the flank near the Arabian peninsula, the area of American oil interests. This eventuality forced the United States to strengthen the position of the Shah and preserve the status quo."[10] Thus the growing tendency in the second Pahlavi era was toward total elimination of pluralism and practice of violence through the army and secret police forces.

One could scarcely have expected a significantly different outcome from the arbitrary rule of the Shah after the fall of Mossadeq and the end of nonviolent parliamentarianism. In the same manner as his father, Reza Khan, Mohammad Reza Shah crushed all hope of democracy and nonviolent pluralism by an iron-willed arbitrary rule. All this was because the regime was founding its legitimacy on the coup of August 1953 which was anything but a lawful act of nonviolent democratization of the Iranian society. Homa Katouzian divides the reign of the Shah into two periods of dictatorship and arbitrary rule. According to him, "From 1963 to 1977 power became concentrated at an accelerating rate because all opposition had been beaten, the oil revenues were accruing to the state at a rapidly increasing (later exploding) rate, and foreign powers, Western as well as Soviet and East European, became increasingly uncritical towards the regime, not least because of the absence of an organized opposition, and the increasing oil wealth."[11] It was not only the Shah and his dictatorial psychology, but also Iran's historical dynamics of violence that prepared the road to the development and acceleration of philosophies of violence among Iranian intellectuals and opponents in the 1960s and 1970s. Both the *Mojahedin-e Khalq* and *Fada'iyan-e Khalq* guerrilla groups played a prominent role in promoting the heroic myth of violent action against the Pahlavi regime. "The Left was not a pro-democracy force in the 1970s; its worldview was collectivist and was not primarily concerned with the rule of law, civil liberties, or individual rights. Rather, it saw the rhetoric of democracy as a means to an end. It was strongly anti-state, favoured class war and revolution, and promised a utopian state."[12]

In the period under question, it was widely believed by the Shah and his political allies that dictatorship was a necessary evil for maintaining state-building in Iran. Therefore, the absence of power sharing which had begun with the coup of 1953 was continued with the process of royal

DOI: 10.1057/9781137330178

autocracy. "Mohammad Reza Shah's justification for his style of government was based on three basic assumptions: the threat of infiltration and subversion from hostile neighbors to the north and west; the masses' incapacity for effective political participation due to illiteracy, poverty, and fanaticism; and the necessity of rapid economic expansion and industrialization free from political and parochial interests."[13] Largely due to its incapacity to analyze the political environment of Iran, the one-man rule of the Shah's regime opened the door to violent guerrilla mentality and radical Islamic opposition.

The two utopias of a classless society and Islamic government became the dominant narratives of dissident thought and action in Pahlavi state. As such, the Shah's political war against Iranian liberalism and the followers of Mossadeq in the 1950s and 1960s resulted in the diminution of nonviolent political discourse and the rise of radical Left and Islamic fundamentalism in pre-revolutionary Iran. As such, the intellectual language of protest against the Shah and his regime was characterized by discourses that were either revivalist or revolutionary. It should be recalled, however, that the Iranian Left was more challenged by the Pahlavi state's security apparatus than some of the Shi'ite clerics and militant groups. "It is important to note that throughout the 1960's and 1970's, while the Left and liberal/social democratic forces and their institutions were hounded and banned by the Pahlavi state, the religious establishment expanded considerably and its institutions proliferated. Networks of mosques, seminaries, and lecture halls, the publication of religious journals and books, access to the print and electronic media, and the steady stream of mullahs (clerics) emerging from the theological schools of Qom and elsewhere provided the leaders of political Islam with an important social base, organization, and resources."[14] The fall and failure of Mossadeq's nationalist-liberal movement and its replacement by Ayatollah Khomeini's radical Islamist protest in 1963 helped to fuel the violent revolutionary mentality. It was in those turbulent years and as an alternative to Pahlavi's monarchy that Ayatollah Khomeini formulated his theory of Islamic government. "In this rather novel theory, during the absence of the prophet's heirs – vacant since the 'great occultation' or disappearance of the twelfth Imam Mahdi in the tenth century – the world can be governed legitimately only by a *Vali-e-Faqih* – the only one who can execute God's will on behalf of the Hidden Imam the agency with the mandate to rule both politically and spiritually."[15]

DOI: 10.1057/9781137330178

ın such social and political configurations under Islamic banners,
ıt would have been difficult to build an anti-Shah intellectual dissent on
anything else but the anti-Western stand of Khomeini (as in the case
of Jalal Al-Ahmad) or on the paradigm of Karbala and the martyrdom
of Imam Hossein as an active demonstration of opposition to Shah's
autocratic regime (Ali Shariati). The principles of Shi'ite Imamate were,
thus, re-interpreted by Iranian intellectuals in order to unify disparate
social categories into one revolutionary movement. Time and time
again, thinkers like Shariati articulated the revolutionary content of
Shi'ism, while making a distinction between a static and passive Islam
and a dynamic Islam. "If we are Muslims, if we are Shi'ites," he affirms,
"and believe in the Islamic and Shi'i precepts, and yet those precepts
have had no positive results upon our lives, it is obvious that we have to
doubt our understanding of them. For we all believe that it is not possible for a nation to be Muslim, to believe in Ali and his way and yet
to gain no benefit from such a belief."[16] To many observers, the success
of the Iranian revolution in 1979 was largely due not only to the political capacities of Ayatollah Khomeini to rally the traditional loyalties of
the masses, but also to the intellectual genius of those who highlighted
the revolutionary elements of Twelver Shi'ism in order to produce a
fundamental paradigm shift from a Western model of modernization to
a model of "national modernity" basically concerned with the purposes
and values of a revolutionary Islam.

Shariati set the standards of revolutionary praxis within the metaphor of martyrdom where "only blood could distinguish the boundary
between truth and falsehood." As such, "Whenever and wherever a
liberated person has refused to submit to despotism and its attempts for
distorting supreme values, and has preferred death to a dehumanized
purposeless existence under a monstrous regime and inhuman social
system, it is a response to Hussein's call. Wherever there is struggle for
liberation, Hussein is present on the battlefield."[17] The same vision was
expressed by Shariati in a speech on the courage of martyrdom: "The
great teacher of martyrdom has risen to teach a lesson to those who
believe that struggle against dictatorship should be waged only when
victory is possible, and to those who have despaired or have compro-
mised with the Establishment, or have become indifferent to their
environment. Hossein teaches that *shahadat* is a *choice* through which a
mujahid, by sacrificing himself on the altar of the temple of freedom and
love, is irrevocably victorious. Hossein has come to teach the Children

DOI: 10.1057/9781137330178

of Adam how to die. He declares that people who submit themselves to all forms of humiliations, injustice and oppression just to live a little longer are destined to die a 'black death.' Those who lack the courage to choose martyrdom, death will choose them."[18] The influence of these ideas on the discourse and praxis of the Iranian revolution can be easily recognized. In other words, Shariati considered the revolutionary praxis as an evolution towards political consciousness and higher moral perfection. For him, revolutionary violence was legitimate as long as it paved the way for the emergence of a radical manifestation of Islamic moral order. However, while popularizing a revolutionary interpretation of Islam Shariati never advocated guerrilla warfare and that is the reason why he was under constant attack from the *Mujahedin-e Khalq* leadership who considered him as an "ivory tower intellectual." But Shariati's theory and that of Al-Ahmad proceeded on parallel lines by emphasizing on an authentic cultural revival of Iranian traditions in opposition to what Al-Ahmad entitled "Occidentosis" or "Westoxication."

Al-Ahmad's critique of the West was accompanied by his argument on a "return" to an "authentic" Iranian culture which was consistent with an Islamic identity. According to Ali Mirsepassi, "With this claim, Al-Ahmad encouraged a belief that the 'good era' of democracy under Mossadeq depended on an alliance of religious and secular politics."[19] As in the case of Ali Shariati, Al-Ahmad's efforts of combating Shah's autocratic regime was followed by a critique of passivity among the clerics added by a celebration of radical Islamic thoughts of Sheikh Nuri and Ayatollah Khomeini. It is interesting to note that Al-Ahmad's meeting with Ayatollah Khomeini in 1964 coincides with his support for Nuri as a "grand martyr" and a critique of the Constitutional Revolution of 1906. Though more an objection of westernization rather than a pure support of Nuri's traditionalism, Al-Ahmad nevertheless criticizes the Constitutional liberals for having executed Nuri and adds: "I look upon that great man's body on the gallows as a flag raised over our nation proclaiming the triumph of Gharbzadegi [Westoxication] after two hundred years of struggle. Under this flag we are like strangers to ourselves, in our food and dress, our homes, our manners, our publications, and most dangerous, our culture... If in the beginning of the Constitutional era the danger brushed up against us, it has now touched our souls-from the peasant who has fled to the city and never returns to his village [to] the minister who seems allergic to the dust of our country and spends the year knocking about the world."[20]

DOI: 10.1057/9781137330178

Al-Ahmad's nativist claim for a return to Iranian cultural identity played an important role in the re-invention of the Iranian political imagination in the pre-revolutionary period of 1970s. Al-Ahmad influenced Iran's contemporary sociocultural debates by presenting the Iranian intellectuals of his time as traitors who wished to be the tool of the democratization process in Iran as did their Western intellectual role models, but since they lived in an undemocratic state (the Shah's), they served the censorship system. Al-Ahmad's clear intention by writing his famous monograph, *Occidentosis*, was not only to incriminate those Iranian intellectuals who viewed "technocratic rationality" as the essence of Western modernity, but to promulgate a new ideological discourse among the "third generation of Iranian intellectuals" that was an amalgamation of Sartre, Heidegger and Fanon. This new ideological discourse symbolized by Al-Ahmad's view of modernity earned him the reputation of a Third-Worldist committed intellectual among the other members of the third generation of Iranian intellectuals. Some even compared Al-Ahmad's "Gharbzadegi" with the Communist Manifesto of Marx and Engels and Fanon's *The Wretched of the Earth* in defining the role of the Iranian nation vis-à-vis the colonialist West.[21] On the other hand, Al-Ahmad's upholding of Shi'ism as Iranians' primordial source of identity against the Western modernity placed him at the center of intellectual debates maintained by scholars such as Naraqi, Nasr, Shariati, Enayat and Shayegan before the Revolution of 1979. Al-Ahmad's ideological view of modernity was an impulse for this generation of Iranian intellectuals to shape their nostalgic dispositions for traditional civilizations. What is most surprising is that while admitting the need for Iranian tradition as the non-West and as a mirror by which the West becomes visible, Iranian intellectuals obviously did not ask if the mirror may be obscure or not. Whether or not the image facilitated by Iranian traditions was the true representation of what was actually there was not at issue.

What is worth noting is that generations of Iranian intellectuals dealt with the Iranian culture and tradition as opposed to the Western traditions as though they were clearly shaped and could be treated exhaustively as objects. All attempts to arrest the strangeness of the other but also the fascination or rejection of the West within Al-Ahmad's "Westoxication" were inevitably undercut by the irreducible affinity for Iranian nationalism and Iranian religious traditions. For over 100 years Iranian intellectuals embraced and appropriated Western political and

DOI: 10.1057/9781137330178

cultural values while at the same time keeping a critical distance from it. Actually in both achieving a discourse on the West and creating a distance from it, they contributed to the creation of a dual sense of magnanimity toward the West coupled with a wounded sense of national pride and a *ressentiment* of the cultural and political intrusion of the West in Iran. The initial romantic "fascination with the West" which took shape among the Iranian intellectuals in the late 19th century was replaced after World War II with a broader romantic "revolt against the West." Surprisingly, the universal sameness of Iranian traditions in opposition to the universal otherness of modernity became a common denominator in both right-wing romantic nationalism and in Marxist anti-imperialist nationalism. In both cases this romance of the authentic cultural and national body was characterized by feelings of cultural relativism and traditional anxiety. Different attempts to generate a sense of national pride triggered by a growing awareness of Iran's backwardness vis-à-vis the West were translated through serious calls for Europeanization, internationalism and pan-Islamism. One must not forget that the sense of nationhood, particularly in contrast with the Western form of temporality, was a useful mechanism of voicing opposition in Iran against different political status quos while being a strong argument for a discourse of "authenticity." As a matter of fact, because of the double structure of romancing and rejecting the West at the same time, a constant oscillation was generated between universalism and particularism among Iranian intellectuals.

Particularism and universalism did not form antimony but rather mutually reinforced each other. The building of an imaginary glorious past under the old Persian kings or the narrating of an utopian Iranian secular or religious society were different modes of particularistic thinking among Iranian intellectuals, which thought of themselves as universalistic without coming across the otherness of the other. One must not forget that all along the 20th century, many Iranian intellectuals joined Arab, Asian and African intellectuals around the world in extolling the virtues of Iranian traditions as a tool for purifying the non-West from the contamination of Western domination. Such romantic resentment was often portrayed as a gesture of emancipation and liberation. For the Iranian intellectualism the "return to roots" and the affirmation of the Perso-Islamic heritage as much as the acquisition of Western knowledge was considered as the protection of one's civilization against outside civilization. In their struggle to overcome modernity, the romantic

DOI: 10.1057/9781137330178

efforts of Iranian intellectuals remained imprisoned in a closed world of cultural solipsism. The metaphor of a frog in the well could be helpful in understanding this problem. The frog can never see its own well on the walls. For the frog, the totality of its well can never be visible. Therefore, it would never know that it is confined to a tiny space; it is not aware that what it believes to be the entire universe is merely a small well. In order to know that its universe is merely a well, the image of the well must be projected on the walls. Thus for the frog the totality of the well is basically invisible and has to be recognized only as a representation projected on the wells.

In a sense, the story of Iranian intellectuals has always been haunted by a sense of insecurity. In other words, preserving Iranian cultural and religious traditions did not necessarily mean isolating oneself from a combination of third-worldism and the movement of counterculture predominant in the West. On the contrary, Iranian intellectuals became endowed with and aware of their own *self* only when they had the feeling that they were recognized by the West. A large number of Iranian intellectuals underlined Iran's particularity on the assumption of Western universalism. It is no accident that the general discourse among Iranian intellectuals on Iranian uniqueness mentions innumerable cases of Iran's difference from the West, thereby defining Iran's identity in terms of deviations from the West. Its insistence on Iran's peculiarity and difference from the West embodies a nagging urge to see the self from the viewpoint of the other. But this is nothing but the positing of Iran's identity in Western terms which in return establishes the centrality of the West as the universal point of reference. In contrast to Turkish cosmopolitanism, meaning the ability of the Turkish intellectuals in 20th century to readily embrace universally applicable attributes of so-called Western civilizational values, Iranian intellectual consciousness combined Iran's Perso-centric and pre-Islamic sense of belonging with Islam as joint foundations of Iranian identity and culture. Yet the existence of these varying perspectives, emerging out of the same national context in Iran, due to encounters with the modern world, point to the very absence of particular instances of "multiple rooted cosmopolitanism" and dialogical encounters with the West among the Iranian intellectuals before the revolution of 1979.

What pre-revolutionary intellectuals in Iran did not understand clearly was that the absence of dialogue with the West did not represent an extension but the destruction of democracy. The irony, alas, was that

DOI: 10.1057/9781137330178

by removing universal standards and declaring that "anything goes," Iranians did not get more democracy, but instead debased imitations of democracy. As such, when hatred of democracy itself became part of a struggle for democracy in Iran, the life of the mind lost all meaning and all hope for a nonviolent change dissipated. Violence as the dominant intellectual project of pre-revolutionary Iran was embodied by the religious and secular segments of the Iranian intelligentsia. At the same time, the nativist attitudes of thinkers like Shariati and Al-Ahmad left plenty of empty space for tradition to become a political statement. As such, the Revolution of 1979 was not so much pro-Islamic as it was pro-traditionalist. Iranians, therefore, turned toward Khomeini as anti-Shah and a critique of modern values. The search for an authoritative tradition was conjoined with a longing for an independent Iran. But the roots of this new dawn of independence were established in a new dynamic of violence in Iranian society. That is to say, the Iranian revolution of 1979 did not come about because of the failure of the Shah's authoritarian rule, but as its direct consequence. The oil boom of the mid-1970s, while creating new economic opportunities for Iran, noticeably revealed its weaknesses by providing liberal measures against political violence.

Pre-revolution Iran was characterized by two distinct sociocultural types of intellectuals: on the one hand, those who were deeply, by leftist reading of modernity and by the communist experience in Iran were, cut from the religious world; and on the other hand, those who believed in Islamic revivalism, but did not feel a philosophical urge to enter a dialogue with modernity. For both of these intellectual categories, the true challenge was to face the paradox of remaining faithful to the critical responsibility of intellectualism while admitting, approving or facing the process of institutionalization of revolutionary Islam as a compelling discourse of power in Iran. In other words, the biggest challenge for many of the liberal and leftist intellectuals was to be able to fulfill their intellectual duty in an anti-intellectual atmosphere characterized by Al-Ahmad's holistic discourse on Westoxication and the "betrayal of intellectuals." Therefore, in the last years of the Pahlavi regime, Iranian intellectuals appeared to be among the weakest elements in the Iranian public sphere.

The Iranian Revolution of February 1979 was a great sociopolitical change with a hybrid synthetic intellectual discourse, but it was undoubtedly not an intellectual change in the direction of a critique of violence in Iran. On the contrary, it was a great political change that heralded

DOI: 10.1057/9781137330178

the return of massive and long-term violence to the annals of modern Iranian history. The rapid downfall of "the strongest power in the Persian Gulf region"[22] followed by the establishment of a dual sovereignty in Iran remains, for many observers and analysts, an unsolved puzzle. The future generations may judge this event and the roles played by Mohammad Reza Shah and Ayatollah Khomeini in a different manner, but while the causes of the Iranian Revolution might be a matter of dispute, there can be no doubt that the collapse of Mossadeq's popular government and the idea of constitutionalism and state of rights opened, once again, the valves of violence in contemporary Iranian history. Whether or not destiny played a part in favor of Ayatollah Khomeini and his followers is not a subject for researchers but a matter of fortune telling. However, what remains clear in the minds of many analysts of Iranian politics and history is the fact that Pahlavi's misconceptions and misreading of Iranian history and the use of violence eventually disintegrated the system. Despite what the supporters of the Shah might say, he was unable to live with the cultural exigencies of urban-educated Iranians and his dream of the Great Civilization for Iran became a typical illusion of a monarch who lived permanently with suspicions and conspiracies. The truth is that "the regime's inability to develop an eclectic Iranian model for development, or to persuade the middle-of-the roaders (if not Islamic traditionalists) of the economic inevitability and clear efficiency of its strategy was the main cause of its failure to gain popular support. The Shah's thesis that his alternative to the Islamic and Marxist models was the only promising one was, for the most part, not widely credible."[23]

In a different but related manner, the Shah's regime exaggerated the role played by the Iranian Communist Party and Marxists intellectuals in Iran. Yet, none of these avowed leftists had the political capacity or the charismatic leadership of spearheading and directing a revolution in the 1970s in Iran. Though most of these radical intellectuals and organizations such as *Feda'iyan-e Khalq* or *Mojahedin Khalq* strongly identified with the use of violence as a legitimate path to end oppression in Iran, they were fully unaware of the boomerang effect of this violence against themselves and their partisans after the revolution of 1979. The fact that these organizations are nowadays contested institutions by Iranian public raises a host of questions about their paramilitary nature during the Shah's regime and how they managed their identity as the wielders of the means of violence. Given their heavy stress on Guevara, Fanon or on Shariati's revolutionary Islam, their general focus was on the victims and

DOI: 10.1057/9781137330178

on the perpetrators of state violence rather than on the violence itself. In suggesting that the means of violence were monopolized by the Pahlavi state, these organizations and intellectuals developed strong feelings about using violence in order to prepare a new society. In practically none of their writings before and after the revolution of 1979 was violence seen as something problematic that had to be constantly controlled. By contrast, violence became an object of fascination and celebration. In this respect, Fanon's *The Wretched of the Earth* became a handbook for all those who were dreaming of putting an end to the Shah's oppressive regime. Fanon's nativist philosophy and his idea of violence as a "cleansing force" and the guerilla warfare experiences of Guevara, Castro and others in Latin America were successful in taking the spirit of young Iranian radicals far from the political and religious realities of Iranian society during the Pahlavi regime and opened the door to a new wave of romanticization of violence as an approach to political struggle in Iran. Although not all military in nature, these narrations and acts of violence nevertheless find their place in the Iran's popular culture of violence. One may argue that whatever the *Feda'iyan* and *Mujahedin* did or did not achieve in their revolutionary struggle against the Pahlavi state, there is no shadow of doubt that as practitioners of violence they exposed Iranian population to the same violence which was justified and used against them by the Islamic Republic after 1979. Thus the guerrilla warfare experience of *Feda'iyan* and *Mujahedin* in 1970s should be seen as one of many political means of popularizing and normalizing violence in contemporary Iran.

On February 8, 1971, a gendarmerie post in Siyahkal in northern Iran was attacked by 13 *Feda'iyan* guerrillas. A few months after this incident which turned into a tragedy for all those who participated in the attack, Mas'ud Ahmadzadeh, one of the founders of the organization and a former member of Mossadeq's National Front, explained the aims of the Siyahkal operation as follows: "The goal of the armed struggle in the beginning was not to inflict a military blow on the enemy but rather a political blow. The aim is to show the path of struggle both to the revolutionaries and to the masses, make them aware of their power, to expose the enemy and awaken the masses."[24] The *Feda'iyan's* heroic acts of violence had a great impact on young, urban-educated Iranians. Interestingly, as in the case of Shariati's writings, we find in the writings and speeches of some Iranian Marxists the reminiscences of the Karbala tragedy and the heroism of Imam Hossein against Yazid, the Ummayid

DOI: 10.1057/9781137330178

caliph. In his self-defense broadcasted on national television in January 1974, Khosrow Golesorkhi, a Marxist poet, likened himself with Imam Hossein, claiming

> The life of Mawla Hossein is an example of our present days when, risking our life for the dispossessed of our country, we are tried in this court. He [Hossein] was in a minority, whereas Yazid had the royal court, the armies, authority, and power. [Hossein] resisted and was martyred. Yazid may have occupied a corner of history, but that which was emulated in history was the way of Mawla Hossein and his resistance, not the rule of Yazid. The [path] that nations have followed and continue to follow is the way of Mawla Hossein. It is in this way that in a Marxist society, real Islam can be justified as a superstructure, and we, too, approve of such an Islam, the Islam of Hossein and Mawla Ali.[25]

As such, the two processes of romanticizing violence and Marxisizing Islam (as in the case of *Mojahedin Khalq*) went hand-in-hand in generating a momentum for the religious opposition to the Shah's regime. The discourse of "religious resistance" as a characteristic of Iranian indigenous culture gained prevalence in response to the Shah's "Americanized culture." It is no wonder then that once the first manifestations of a religious violence began in 1979, advocating the cause of an Islamic sovereignty and the Shari'a law, many secular intellectuals and political activists did not question the roots and reasons of this violence. Instead they found it natural and rewarding to give their full benediction.

Future Iranian generations will find it hard to believe that Ayatollah Khomeini succeeded in establishing a violent theocracy in Iran in the later decades of the 20th century on a violent stage framed and normalized by Mohammad Reza Shah and his Marxist opponents. Looking back in time, one needs to underline that Ayatollah Khomeini, unlike Iranian Leftists, did not romanticize violence but practiced it in an unbending manner against his enemies. "Paradoxically, both Mohammad Reza Shah and Ayatollah Khomeini considered themselves agents of the will of God,"[26] but Iranians saw in the latter the image of a Shi'ite Imam who would free Iran from injustice and corruption. The monumental misunderstanding, however, was that the main goal for Ayatollah Khomeini was not to establish freedom and nonviolence, but to end with the Constitutional Revolution of 1906. In the same manner as Sheikh Nuri 70 years before, Ayatollah Khomeini declared: "The Constitution is not the last word for us. Whatever is contrary to the Qur'an we shall oppose, even the Constitution."[27] This tendency to raise the violent voice of an

DOI: 10.1057/9781137330178

authoritative religious tradition as the "legitimate" and "authentic" culture of Iran gave everyone in the early days of the Revolution an idea of what the Islamic Republic would look like. To rephrase the famous quote by George Orwell, Ayatollah Khomeini and his followers did not establish an Islamic theocracy in order to safeguard a revolution; they made a revolution in order to establish an Islamic theocracy. But in doing so, they took the genie of violence out of the bottle, the same genie which had been put back in the bottle by the Constitutional Revolution of 1906 and during Mossadeq's premiership. Those who made Mossadeq's nonviolent reforms impossible did not know that they were guiding Iranian society towards tremendous, inexorable violence 25 years later.

Notes

1 Fakhreddin Azimi, "Unseating Mossadeq: The Configuration and Role of Domestic Forces," M.J. Gasiorowski and M. Byrne, *Mohammad Mossadeq and the 1953 Coup in Iran*, Syracuse: Syracuse University Press, 2004, p. 30.

2 Ibid., p. 72.

3 M.J. Gasiorowski, "Why Did Mossadeq Fall?" M.J. Gasiorowski and M. Byrne, *Mohammad Mossadeq and the 1953 Coup in Iran*, Syracuse: Syracuse University Press, 2004, pp. 267–268.

4 Azimi, "Unseating Mossadeq", p. 66.

5 Quoted by Sohrab Behdad, "Navvab Safavi and the Feda'ian-e Eslam in Prerevolutionary Iran," *Iran: Between Tradition and Modernity*, ed. Ramin Jahanbegloo, Maryland: Lexington Books, 2004, p. 80.

6 N. Marbury Efimenco, "An Experiment with Civilian Dictatorship in Iran: The Case of Mohammed Mossadegh," *The Journal of Politics* 17(1955): 404.

7 Efimenco, "An Experiment with Civilian Dictatorship in Iran," p. 405.

8 Ibid., p. 404.

9 Homa Katouzian, "Mossadeq's Government in Iranian History: Arbitrary Rule, Democracy and the 1953 Coup," M.J. Gasiorowski and M. Byrne, *Mohammad Mossadeq and the 1953 Coup in Iran*, Syracuse: Syracuse University Press, 2004, p. 20.

10 Efimenco, "An Experiment with Civilian Dictatorship in Iran", pp. 405–406

11 Homa Katouzian, *Iranian History and Politics: The Dialectic of State and Society*, London: Routledge, 2003, p. 110.

12 Gheissari, Ali and Vali Nasr, *Democracy in Iran: History and the Quest for Liberty*, Oxford: Oxford University Press, 2006, p. 67

13 Jahangir Amuzegar, *The Dynamics of the Iranian Revolution: The Pahlavis' Triumph and Tragedy*, New York: State University of New York Press, 1991, p. 125.

DOI: 10.1057/9781137330178

14   Ali Mirsepassi, *Intellectual Discourse and the Politics of Modernization:*
      Negotiating Modernity in Iran, Cambridge: Cambridge University Press, 2000,
      p. 163.
15   Amuzegar, *The Dynamics of the Iranian Revolution*, 27.
16   Quoted in Mangol Bayat-Phillip, "Shi'ism in Contemporary Iranian Politics:
      The Case of Ali Shari'ati," Elie Kedourie and Sylvia G. Haim, *Towards a*
      Modern Iran, London: Frank Cass, 1980, p. 156.
17   Quoted in Suroosh Irfani, *Revolutionary Islam in Iran*, London: Zed Books,
      1983, pp. 131–132.
18   Ibid., p. 133.
19   Mirsepassi, *Intellectual Discourse and the Politics of Modernization*, p. 106.
20   Jalal Al-Ahmad, *Occidentosis: A Plague from the West*, trans. R. Campbell,
      Berkeley: Mizan Press, 1984, pp. 57–58.
21   This view was expressed by Reza Baraheni in *Qessehnevissi*, 2nd ed. (Tehran:
      Ashrafi, 1969), quoted in Mehrzad Boroujerdi, *Iranian Intellectuals and the*
      West: The Tormented Triumph of Nativism, Syracuse: Syracuse University Press,
      1996, p. 67.
22   This term was used in a major study by George Lenczowski entitled *Iran*
      Under the Pahlavis, Stanford: Hoover institution Press, 1978.
23   Amuzegar, *The Dynamics of the Iranian Revolution*, p.207.
24   Mas'ud Ahmadzadeh, *Mobarezeh-ye mosallahaneh, ham Esteratezhi ham Taktik*
      (*Armed Struggle, Both a Strategy and a Tactic*), Sazman-e Jebheh-ye Melli-ye
      Kharej az Kheshvar, quoted in Buroujerdi, *Iranian Intellectuals and the West*,
      p. 35.
25   Quoted in Negin Nabavi, "The Discourse of 'Authentic Culture' in Iran in the
      1960s and 1970s," ed. Negin Nabavi, *Intellectual Trends in Twentieth-Century*
      Iran: A Critical Survey, Miami: University Press of Florida, Miami, 2003, p. 91.
26   Amuzegar, *The Dynamics of the Iranian Revolution*, p. 113.
27   Quoted in Amuzegar, *The Dynamics of the Iranian Revolution*, p. 120.

DOI: 10.1057/9781137330178

5

The Two Sovereignties and Islamist Violence in Iran

Abstract: *The crises and decline of liberal institutions left a political vacuum, which provided the opportunity for political Islam to organize and mobilize the population. Once in power, the forces of Islam formulated a new ideology, velayat-e faqih, which claimed that every individual required religious guardianship. Following this ideology, the new regime structured government in such a way that it emphasized the divine clerical-rights of the religious leaders, and the people's authority and rights (the latter becoming increasingly symbolic). Although the new constitution established a unicameral parliament, presided by an elected president, the overwhelming power was situated in the office of the Supreme Leader. Merely a decade after the revolution, Iran's political system began experiencing a disintegration of popular sovereignty and ongoing crises of legitimacy.*

Jahanbegloo, Ramin. *Democracy in Iran*. Basingstoke: Palgrave Macmillan, 2013. DOI: 10.1057/9781137330178.

The rise of political Islam in the course of the Iranian Revolution was not a historically pre-determined phenomenon, nor an accident. The crisis and decline of liberal institutions resulted in a political vacuum in Iran and provided an ideal opportunity for the Islamic forces to organize themselves and mobilize the population.

Ayatollah Khomeini elaborated and established the ideology of *velayat-e faqih*, which claimed that Muslims, in fact everyone, required "guardianship" in the form of rule or supervision by the leading Islamic jurist or jurists – such as Khomeini himself. Under these conditions, Islamic jurists were meant to exclusively follow Shari'a law, thus protecting Islam from innovation and deviation. Such rule was believed to prevent poverty, injustice, and external influence in Islamic matters. The Assembly of Experts fashioned a constitution that created the office of Supreme Leader, a powerful post for Khomeini, who was at that time leading military and security forces and had the power to appoint top officers within the government and judiciary. The weaker office of the president was to be filled by popular election every four years.[1] The Council of Guardians was created to provide another theocratic level of government. This council had the authority to veto candidates seeking to become president, members of parliament, the Assembly of Experts (the organization that elects the Supreme Leader), and even legislation passed by the parliament.

The Iranian Revolution was a shock felt around the world. In the non-Muslim world, it generated a renewed interest in Islamic religion and politics. For Muslims, it was seen as a triumph for Islam and reinvigorated resistance to Western influences and interventions. It inspired the 1979 takeover of the Grand Mosque in Saudi Arabia, the assassination of Egyptian President Sadat in 1981, the Hama Massacre in Syria, and the 1983 bombings of the American embassy in Lebanon. Of the existing Islamic states, Iran is the most interesting case but also the most problematic to consider. For instance, "Iran is the only example of an Islamic state installed through a popular revolution."[2] This is why there is a dualism in the structures of the Islamic Republic of Iran. The duality is not only indicated in the very title of the Islamic Republic which refers to an elected republican body with a president and a parliament functioning in the same political structure with the rule of a *faqih*, but it also relates to the fact that the Islamic Republic declares the unity and brotherhood of all Muslims in one *Umma* and yet reinforces Iranian nationalism. In this sense, the concept of the government of the jurist, whereby the

DOI: 10.1057/9781137330178

state is largely an administrative arrangement to implement the Shari'a, was only one element in Khomeini's understanding of the nature of the state. He also saw it as vested in the model of a philosopher ruler, with a wisdom and knowledge that is higher than the law. But Khomeini's understanding of authority had to come to terms with modern understandings derived from the West.[3] The result has been a constitution which gives predominance to Shari'a and authority based on the divine will, but also incorporates the will of the people and their sovereignty. This mixture has produced many contradictions, particularly in terms of parliamentary legislation conflicting with Shari'a and the authority of the jurist overriding legitimate constitutional structures. Thus the Revolution created a popular support for the state, but on the basis of two conflicting principles of sovereignty.

Iran's constitution is, therefore, in reality two constitutions: one which emphasizes people's authority and rights and another that is a divine clerical-rights constitution. Any debate about the power structure of the Islamic regime in Iran and the struggle among different institutions hinges upon how this dichotomy is perceived and practiced. This is to say that politics in the Islamic Republic of Iran are characterized by fierce competitiveness among power groups.

As mentioned, the highest official within the Iranian political structure is the office of Supreme Leader, which is currently held by Ayatollah Khomeini's successor, Ayatollah Ali Khamenei. Khamenei is responsible for delineation and supervision of "the general policies of the Islamic Republic of Iran," meaning that he sets the tone and direction of Iran's domestic and foreign policies. He is the commander-in-chief of the armed forces and he controls the intelligence and the security. He also has the power to appoint and dismiss the leaders of the judiciary, the state broadcasting networks and the supreme commander of the Revolutionary Guards. He also appoints 6 of the 12 members of the Council of Guardians. The Council of Guardians is vested with the authority to interpret the constitution and determine if the laws passed by the Parliament are in line with the Shari'a. Hence, he has a veto power over the Parliament. The council also examines presidential and parliamentary candidates to determine their legitimacy to run for a seat. In the latest presidential elections in Iran only 8 of over 2000 candidates were allowed to go on the ballot paper. The Assembly of Experts, which meets for one week every year, in turn elects the Supreme Leader, but it also supervises the activities of the Leader and all the organizations

DOI: 10.1057/9781137330178

controlled by his office. The assembly consists of 86 "virtuous and learned" clerics elected by the public to eight-year terms. Many analysts compare the Assembly of Experts to the Vatican's College of Cardinals.

In 1988, Ayatollah Khomeini created the Expediency Council, which has the authority to mediate disputes between the two bodies of the Council of Guardians and the Parliament. The Supreme Leader appoints each member of the Expediency Council, which in turn serves as an advisory body to the Supreme Leader. The Iranian Parliament is a unicameral legislative body with 290 members elected by the public every four years. Each member of the Parliament represents a geographic constituency. The Parliament introduces and passes laws that are ultimately checked and approved by the Council of Guardians. The Parliament is also responsible for impeaching Cabinet ministers and for approving the country's budget. Last but not least, the president is the second highest-ranking figure in Iran. Elected by popular vote to a four-year term, the president appoints and supervises the Cabinet and coordinates government decisions. The president is also responsible for setting the country's economic policies, but does not control the armed forces. As a matter of fact, though the president has a nominal authority over the Supreme National Security Council and the Ministry of Intelligence, in practice the Supreme Leader controls all matters of security. The constitutional amendments of 1988, which appeared to consolidate presidential authority, in fact granted the Supreme Leader and institutions related to him unhindered power.

In contrast to the formal institutions of power, the informal power structure consists of revolutionary organizations, the foundations (Bonyads), the IRGC (Revolutionary Guards), the Basij militia, security forces and the media. Therefore, all of Iran's power structure is controlled by the Islamic revolutionary elite – composed of Shi'i clerics and laypersons – who nevertheless do not have a monopoly of power over the practice of politics in Iran. In fact, there are numerous political groups and personalities that are located in the gray zone between the regime and the civil society. Many of them such as Abdolkarim Sorush, Ezatollah Sahabi or Ibrahim Yazdi held influential positions in the regime during the first years of the Revolution, but they were subsequently forced to the margins of the system. Among these, Ayatollah Hossein Ali Montazeri played an important role because, unlike the quietist clerics of Qom or Mashhad (who advocate the withdrawal of clerics from politics), he accepted the concept of *velayat-e faqih* in principle but rejected Ayatollah

DOI: 10.1057/9781137330178

Khamenei's credentials for this position. However, Ayatollah Montazeri later challenged the absolutist version of the *velayat-e faqih* while remaining loyal to Khomeini's theory.

This is the panorama for the ongoing struggle of power in Iran. The election of Mohammad Khatami to the office of president initiated a new phase in the evolution of the power struggle in the Islamic Republic of Iran. Khatami's landslide election in 1997 was a positive step in transition to popular sovereignty in that it drew the support of a younger generation of voters and placed a renewed focus on political pluralism. Iran's youth, many previously too young to vote or alienated from the political system, made up a large part of the 20 million who gave Khatami his surprise victory. Both the younger generations and newly politicized women saw Khatami as an agent for social and political change. That they believed they could achieve change by means of the existing political system speaks well for the existing contradictions inside the Iranian political system. As for Khatami, he used Islamic vernacular and nationalistic symbols to articulate a new discourse of governance in Iran based on popular sovereignty. It can hardly be contested that Khatami's election and his eight years of presidency popularized the discourse of democracy in Iran and opened once again the debate about democratization in Iran.

However, Mahmoud Ahmadinejad's victory took everyone, both inside and outside of Iran, by surprise, ushering in a new era of ultra-conservative politics. Many projected that Hashemi Rafsanjani was ahead in that election and was assured of success. But what is totally unprecedented is that as a result of this election, for the first time in the life of the Islamic Republic, virtually every organ and institution of power, electable or otherwise, has been handed over to the complete control of the ultra-conservatives. Ahmadinejad has retained important political assets. Arguably most significant is the nationalist fervor born of Iran's nuclear program. While Khatami, his predecessor, was criticized for being overly passive and conciliatory, Ahmadinejad is blamed for being too adventurous in his aggressive tone toward Israel and in his Holocaust-denial discourse. Ahmadinejad has proved himself a populist throughout most of his tenure, but he has come under heightened criticism over his economic policies. Such criticism has lead to increased public disapproval of Ahmadinejad's political program. This disapproval has even come from conservatives who have grown increasingly critical of Ahmadinejad's capacity to effectively manage the nuances of Iran's

DOI: 10.1057/9781137330178

political and economic foundations. What is forgotten, however, is that Iran today is very much like the Soviet Union in its last days. Attempts to reform the system from within have failed, the leading ideology has increasingly lost popular support, and groups such as the youth and women are becoming motivated to participate in public disobedience against the government. This has lead to an escalation of public protest and civil unrest throughout Iran.

Ever since the first days of the Islamic Republic of Iran, there have been two sovereignties – the divine and the popular. The concept of popular sovereignty, which is derived from the indivisible will of the Iranian nation, is inscribed in Article I of the constitution of the Islamic Republic. And the divine concept of sovereignty, which is derived from God's will through the medium of Shi'i institutions of an Imamate, is bestowed on the existing *faqih* as the rightful ruler of the Shi'ite community, a perception that forms the foundation of the doctrine of the *velayat-e faqih*.[4] Increasingly, divine sovereignty has been less about religion than about political theology. As for the popular sovereignty, it has found its due place in social networks and political action of Iranian civil society. The presence of these two incompatible and conflicting conceptions of sovereignty, authority and legitimacy have always been a bone of contention in Iranian politics, often defining the ideological contours of the political power struggle among contending forces. The present crisis in Iran following the Iranian presidential elections is rooted in the popular quest for the democratization of the state and society and the conservative reaction and opposition to it. But there is another factor distinguishing the current political crisis from the previous instances of political factionalism and internal power struggles in Iran.

Thirty years after the revolts that did away with the Shah and his regime, there is an absence of an organizational factor to unite the diverse inspirations of Iranians. Whether the Islamic Republic evolves into more of a democracy or will crumble in revolution is anyone's guess. For the vast majority of Iranians living inside the country, a people who are already disenchanted with one revolution and have suffered from a brutal eight-year war with Iraq, peaceful evolution is a more favorable option. For the younger generation, the 70 percent of the population under the age of 30, the change has to come sooner or later because they are looking for jobs, social freedom and opportunity.

So the practical problem the Islamic Republic faces can be interpreted along two poles: on the one hand, subjecting practical problems to so

DOI: 10.1057/9781137330178

much religious dispute that solving the practical problem becomes secondary, and on the other hand, the danger of secularizing Iranian society. Secularization is less apparent in domestic politics, however, where a strict Islamic system is still enforced, and no political parties, factions or candidates other than those supporting the system, are allowed into the political arena. So, as long as the constitution remains in force, Islamic republicanism will have practical difficulties and the tension between the "republican" and the "Islamic" will continue. The crisis in Iran, therefore, is not simply between Mousavi and Ahmadinejad; it is not an opposition between the pragmatics and the utopians or between reformists and conservatives. It is basically over how the political agency and political sphere are defined in Iran. In other words, "It is about what is to be done, how it is to be done, by whom it is to be done, and with what means it is to be done."[5] What we have been witnessing for over a year in Iran is a conflict between the realm of politics, which aims at an absolute sovereignty through the practice of violence and the realm of the political, or rather, the popular agency in the public sphere. Through massive participation in the presidential elections and later by protesting against the results of the elections, many representatives of the Iranian civil society were not only trying to refute the legitimacy of the sovereignty but also to discover the better angels of their social nature and try to form and express their moral capital. The level of future success in the democratization of Iranian society is closely related to the level of moral capital expressed and practiced by Iranian civil society.

Those who seek to repudiate the Iranian regime's equation of truth with itself, knowingly or not, have started to slowly and subtly reject the "life of a lie." Iran, with its young population, has become a society that has achieved moral and political progress through its ability to understand the motives and meanings of dissent as a resistance to unjust laws. The ongoing protests in Iran demonstrated that resistance against unjust laws has become not only a way of life but the only way to survive as a nation. This means that in these uncertain and dangerous times, with the air in Iran filled with the idea of plots and conspiracy theories, Iranian civil society has found the urge to struggle for democratic legitimacy. The foundation of this legitimacy is a moral capital that could have a certain weight in Iranian politics at a time of serious crisis. It is interesting to underline that while the Iranian political structure is going through a crisis of legitimacy and current power-holders have lost moral credibility by virtue of misgovernment and lying in politics, the Iranian civil society

DOI: 10.1057/9781137330178

is redefining its legitimacy by re-founding and refining its republican principles.

The republican gesture in Iran pays attention almost exclusively to the legitimacy of the public space in opposition to the political theology that is represented and expressed by the absolute sovereignty of the *faqih*. It is true that the presence of these two incompatible and conflicting conceptions of legitimacy have always been a bone of contention in Iranian politics, often defining the ideological contours of the political power struggle among contending forces, but the present crisis is over a deep-seated legal and political legitimacy and a moral capital that Ayatollah Khomeini had created with his charismatic authority at the time of the Iranian Revolution. Even at critical times, like the war against Iraq, this moral capital tipped the balance between hope and belief, or at least gave Ayatollah Khomeini the foothold he needed to build stability and security for the Iranian regime. Today, the equation between charismatic moral capital and institutional moral capital is widely absent in the Iranian political system. The second life of the Islamic Republic from the 1990s onwards opened up a credibility gap in the political life of the Islamic regime and initiated a long-term mistrust of the political institutions and the principle of theocratic sovereignty. The crisis of legitimacy that is often said to have afflicted the Iranian political system since the 1990s was a crisis of which Rafsanjani, Khatami and Ahmadinejad have been, in important ways, as much symptoms as causes. Also implicated in this crisis were the entire government and its various agencies, the Iranian society and the citizens themselves, and the founding myth of the Iranian Revolution, as upholding popular sovereignty, to which they had held for so long. The crisis was, to put it rather grandly, a crisis of the Iranian Revolution and a sharp divide between popular sovereignty and authoritarian rule at the heart of the Islamic Republic's political framework. Iran had emerged from its revolution in 1979 with its faith in its own goodness reaffirmed by the defeat of the Shah and the war against Saddam. But the heroic stamp and the revolutionary fervor steadily gave way to disillusionment and cynicism.

Three spheres of dissent discourse have thrived in post-revolutionary Iran. They include women, youth and intellectuals. These three spheres of dissent have each embodied deliberate and conscious forms of resistance against absolute sovereignty within Iran. Iranian women have been struggling for more freedom in both the public and private spheres. As for the Iranian intellectuals, they have been highlighting, in the past 20

DOI: 10.1057/9781137330178

years, democratic accountability and value-pluralism as foundations for empowering and enlarging Iranian civil society. One needs to add the Iranian youth to the list of dissenting sociological actors. They belong to a new generation that did not experience the revolution of 1979 and wants another Iran. Most of them were not around or are too young to remember the revolution, but they made up one-third of the eligible voters in the presidential election. But due to the hegemonic political discourse and forced Islamization, an alternative and rebellious youth culture emerged that has been increasingly a part of a larger global cultural movement.

It goes without saying that the Iranian civil society has been quite vibrant and path-breaking despite theocratic sovereignty in Iran. Therefore, there has been simultaneously a popular quest for the democratization of the state and society, and a violent conservative reaction and opposition to it.

As such, one can consider the election of Mahmoud Ahmadinejad in 2005 as the final step in a progressive shift in the Iranian revolution from popular republicanism to absolute theocratic sovereignty. In their way, Ahmadinejad and his group gave themselves the task of closing the chapter of popular sovereignty by giving a new life to the authoritarian structure of the Islamic republic and removing any space for dissent. The republic that Ahmadinejad represented in his person and with his presidency was in a very unusual way theocratic and anti-republican.

The presidential election of 2009 was the only remaining political sphere where the Iranian nation could express its disillusionment and dissatisfaction and test its republican virtue. At stake was the moral capital of the Iranian nation itself insofar as participation in the public sphere informed the nation's sense of its own rightness and grounded its morale. Moreover, it was a way for the Iranian citizens to reconfirm their status as natural actors in the Iranian public sphere and to ask politicians to uphold a truthful mirror to the nation. The recent events in Iran showed the world that a political system which turns into a Hobbesian form of absolute sovereignty is incapable of having truthful mirror-holders because such a state is not in the business of "living in truth" and fostering transparency; it speaks and uses daggers.

Despite Ahmadinejad's formal swearing-in as president of Iran, street demonstrations against his presidency continued. After several months of post-election turmoil, hundreds were killed or jailed. The dominant methods of the regime to quell the unrest have included intimidation,

DOI: 10.1057/9781137330178

censorship, arrests, confessions and, of course, warnings to other nations not to interfere in Iran's "internal affairs." The same tone was part of the standard rhetoric of all communist dictatorships, and the military dictatorship in Latin America back in the 1970s. As John Travis has noted, "More than 240 other prominent Iranian lawyers, activists, journalists, professors, human rights defenders, and students who have been arrested without warrants at their homes or places of work by unidentified agents and taken to undisclosed locations."[6] The authorities in Iran have driven protestors from the streets by deploying police and Basij militia in almost every major square in Tehran and other cities. It is true that the popular demonstrations in Iran demonstrated the great bravery of a people as they confronted the Basij militia, but it is also true that the Revolutionary Guard and the security forces have both shown the willingness and capability to violently cracking down on peaceful protesters. The emerging power dynamics leave protestors with tough choices. If they continue informing the Iranian rulers of their lawful rights through nonviolent demonstrations they would certainly increase the influence of the military and security forces and risk bloodshed. But if they put an end to their movement of civil disobedience because of the harsh repression they might lose the support and sympathy of the outside world.

The "trials" of more than a hundred reformists were a reminder of the Moscow show trials of 1936–1938 where the Old Bolsheviks, like Zinoviev and Bukharin – major figures in the October Revolution – were accused of counter-revolutionary activity, sabotage, murder and collaboration with fascism. As in the Moscow trials, which coincided with the final climax of Stalin's Great Purges, the Tehran trials are a public symbol of a coup against some of the architects of the revolution, accused now of promoting a "velvet revolution" in Iran. For Stalin, the Moscow trials were a means of shifting the blame for the unpopularity of his regime on to scapegoats who might otherwise have supplanted him. By accusing his opponents of espionage, terror and causing all the ills of the Soviet regime, Stalin made the lie big enough to stick. Here, the "confessions" from those on trial are designed to support the allegations by senior government officials that Iran's post-election protests were supported by foreign powers and aimed at overthrowing the government, as well as shutting down disputes over the election's legitimacy. The confessions, almost certainly produced under harsh interrogation, beatings, sleep deprivation, and threats of torture, are also meant to frighten Iranian reformers and civil society activists, including top-ranking political

DOI: 10.1057/9781137330178

figures such as opposition candidate Mir Hossein Mousavi and the two former presidents, Mohammad Khatami and Ali Akbar Rafsanjani. Iranian civil society may have lost an election. It may have lost the public sphere. But Iranian citizens certainly learned that if they were going to build the house of Iran's future, strong and secure, but also honest and beautiful, they would need to dig deep for the ethical foundations. The Iranian public space is faced, then, with the problem of combining a rejection of absolute sovereignty with the need to put faith in a challenge "from below" – in the independent life of "civil society" outside the frame of state power. This, of course, resides in the self-organization of Iranian civil society that defies the violence embodied in the Iranian state and its instruments of control and domination. But it is also closely related to new ethical standards against which Iranian political reality could be measured. By assuming an ethical stance, the Iranian civil society can make a stronger political case. In a violent political society like Iran in which most of the ethical values have been largely discarded, the notion of nonviolent action needs once again to be highlighted. Violence is after all violence, even if it holds up the banner of populism with a cover-up of religious institutions.

There is no way today for Iranian civil society to fight against lies in Iranian politics without holding to the truth of nonviolence. "Today, Mousavi has become the symbol of nonviolent protest in Iran, but the true hero of the Iranian civic movement is the emerging republican model of nonviolent resistance and non-ideological politics that provide the clearest guideline and vision for Iran's gradual transition to democracy."[7] Over the past 30 years, post-revolutionary Iran has seen two political projects at the heart of the 1979 Revolution fail in both practice and in theory: revolutionarism and ideological Islam. While these qualities once rallied the people and claimed a basis of legitimacy, they are increasingly falling out of favor with the broader citizenry.

It is evident that nonviolent action is the new paradigm that is attempting to define itself distinctly and overcome the intellectual and political weaknesses of its predecessors. There is common agreement among the members of Iranian civil society that the main contradiction in contemporary Iran is the one between authoritarian violence and democratic nonviolence. Though this nonviolent paradigm is still in the making, it can nonetheless be characterized as "post-ideological." This is due to the fact that the protest movement in Iran is nonviolent and civil in its methods of creating social change while also seeking an ethical dimension to

DOI: 10.1057/9781137330178

Iranian politics. This judgment implies that Iranian civil society is ready to make a distinction between two approaches: searching for truth and solidarity versus lying and using violence. The question of whether the elections were or were not rigged is now a secondary issue. What is now at stake is to challenge the illegitimacy of violence in Iran. Today, the most difficult challenge of Iranian civil society is to face the violence of the dominant political system without descending into violence. Many believe that it is not possible to turn the Iranian political system around through nonviolent action. That may be the case. But in the words of Daniel Berrigan, "one thing favors such an attempt: the total inability of violence to change anything for the better." And as Gandhi once said: "You must be the change you wish to see in the world."[8] In the past years, many Iranians have shown the world that they have enough maturity and tolerance to be the nonviolent change in Iran.

Notes

1   http://www.iranonline.com/iran/iran-info/Government/constitution.html

2   Sami Zubaida, "An Islamic State? The Case of Iran," *Middle East Report* 153 (1988), p. 4

3   See Ruhollah Khomeini, *Islam and Revolution: Writing and Declarations of Imam Khomeini*, ed. and trans. Hamid Algar (Berkeley: Mizan Press, 1981).

4   Asghar Schirazi, *The Constitution of Iran: Politics and the State in the Islamic Republic*, New York: I.B. Tauris, 1997.

5   John Kane, *The Politics of Moral Capital*, New York: Cambridge University Press, 2001, p. 277.

6   See John x, "Iranian-American Academic Detained in Tehran," *University World News*, (August 2, 2009).

7   Amitabh Pal, "Islamic Nonviolence: The Iranian Example," *The Amana Media Initiative*, http://www.arf-asia.org/amana/prod/index.php?option=com_content&task=view&id=3421&Itemid=98.

8   Printed in Gandhi, "The Indian Opinion on September, 8, 1913," Vol. 13, p. 241.

DOI: 10.1057/9781137330178

Part II
Democratic Nonviolence: The New Imperative

▶

DOI: 10.1057/9781137330178

6
Struggle for Democracy in Iran

Abstract: *If Iran is to reclaim the public sphere and embrace democracy, then society must organize itself behind nonviolence. Peace and nonviolent values are particularly strong amongst the Iranian youth, and as was witnessed in the pro-democratic Green Movement, wider civil society has also began to embrace these values. Only through nonviolent struggle can the Iranian civil society offer a direct and effective contradiction to the violence of the regime. For nonviolent discourse to be effective, however, a transnational unified front consisting of intellectuals, social activists and women must exist.*

Jahanbegloo, Ramin. *Democracy in Iran*. Basingstoke: Palgrave Macmillan, 2013. DOI: 10.1057/9781137330178.

DOI: 10.1057/9781137330178

Gandhi believed that human destiny has constantly been on the move toward nonviolence. Gandhi's practice and perfection of nonviolence testified that where challenges and issues manifest themselves on the roadmap of human destiny, humanity has no choice but to continue striving for nonviolence despite the challenges and issues. It is true that this view is challenged by new forms of conflict and violations of human rights in today's world. Contemporary Iranian society has scarcely been able to fit itself into a nonviolent mode of social and political organization. However, within a society like Iran where there are sharp cleavages between the wealthy and the poor and clashes between the traditional and the modern, there is a strong potential for nonviolent change in the Iranian civil society which we must now seriously consider. It is true that there is still a possibility for violent clashes and for armed conflict to take place in Iranian society, but it is also true that peace and nonviolence are among the core values of the Iranian youth, stemming from the society 's current democratic priorities.

The crackdown on Iran's pro-democracy Green Movement showed us that the universality of nonviolence is not always effective against the dominating will of one man or a group of men in power. However, what is also showed us is that there is a growing awareness among Iranian civil society of the need to go beyond this violence. One can suggest that although violence has come to be accepted as the dominant characteristic of Iranian politics in the present, there is also considerable evidence to suggest that nonviolence is a strong element in the refashioning of political culture in Iran's future. In other words, nonviolence is viewed in a new perspective informed by a reappraisal of the new challenges of Iran's political future in order to make it more effective. This new perspective and this reappraisal are essentially the functions of practice and learning of nonviolence in Iran. All this amounts to saying that a new learning in nonviolence means a whole paradigm shift in the question of Iranian politics. A change in the guiding principles of Iranian politics is basic to a change in the principles that guide the life of Iranian nation.

Nonviolence and Iranian public consciousness, in today's Iranian political context, is one of the most difficult pairs of ideas to reconcile. Like most countries in the process of democratization in general and Islamic countries in particular, modern Iranian culture and politics can be interpreted to have endorsed violence as well as nonviolence. The term "nonviolence" is itself a new concept in the Iranian public sphere though, as it was previously shown, Iranians have been involved

DOI: 10.1057/9781137330178

publicly and politically for the past 100 years with the two concepts of "rule of law" and "social justice." However, in contradistinction from the previous social and political movements in Iran, which insisted one way or another on the primacy of violent struggle against dictatorships, the centrality of nonviolence is paramount in the work of Iranian civil society in the post-revolutionary period of 1990–2010. It is true that the work of Iranian civil society remained a minority, but it is also true that its political and philosophical influences upon the development of the Iranian public sphere towards nonviolent action have been beyond all proportion. The brutal policies of the Iranian government in the past three decades have convinced many that the tyrannical rule in Iran would only end in a violent showdown, and to that end some political groups inside and outside the country believe in having an active military wing. Nonetheless, the heart of the Iranian civil society has been classic nonviolent resistance: education, vigils, rallies, marches, petitions, boycotts, fasts and civil disobedience. Governmental attempts to stop this resistance with massive detentions and imprisonment, banning of organizations, shutting down of journals, intimidation and murder have not stopped the nonviolent movement.

The system has tried in the past to absorb some forms of civil society into the structures of the state. The failure to do that was one of the catalysts that led to the emergence of a number of independent groups and the atmosphere which precipitated the making of the Green movement in 2009. All those who have rejected Islamic theocracy and the encompassing domination of the clergy and revolutionary guards in all its institutional forms have subscribed to what can be called "solidarity of truth." As such, the goal for many civil society activists has been not only to drive the system out of their personal lives, but also to promote nonviolent values such as building gender equality, respecting the opponent's humanity, struggling against the culture of lying, encouraging truth seeking and forgiveness, and slowly preparing conditions for the emergence of a democratic, pluralistic, self-organizing civil society which by its existence would limit political power. For one thing, the civil society structures in Iran have involved radically decentralized and non-pyramidical struggles in which each individual has been at the center of nonviolent action. The rationale of such an action is derived from the nonviolent imperative that all those in the Iranian civil society who maintained a proper balance between nonviolent resistance and constructive work ought to take part in the nonviolent process of

DOI: 10.1057/9781137330178

change. It goes without saying that a brief study of the work of Iranian civil society in the past 20 years confirms clearly its capacity to generate and articulate ideas and values and to create civic solidarities among Iranian citizens that have helped start a democratic impulse in Iran. This is where the debate on the democratic future of Iran belongs. It cannot be disposed of by assumed cultural taboos imposed upon Iranians by their past, which has generated much violence and hatred. Living through two revolutions, one coup d'état, one armed occupation and sporadic guerilla warfare in one century, several generations of Iranians have learned far more than other Middle Easterners about the destructiveness and horrors of violence. In this context, the legacy of Iranian civil society is not only an important milestone in its own history, but also an important milestone in the history of nonviolent initiative for democracy in Iran. It seems that the role of civil society in the process of political and social change in Iran in the past two decades has evolved from an ad hoc strategy associated with religious or ethical principles into a reflective and organized method of struggle in the Green Movement.

Indeed, the past 20 years have witnessed a remarkable upsurge in nonviolent thinking and civic action against autocratic rule in Iran. Civil society and nonviolent action, more than any other topics, have been subjects of intense debate and contention in Iran in the past decades. It was Iranian civil society that produced the post-electoral events in June 2009 and no one, inside or outside Iran, predicted such a major shift in Iranian politics before it happened. To the casual observer, this debate on civil society may sound like a barren intellectual exercise with little or no relevance to the harsh realities of political life. Indeed, some even argue that Iran's repressive regime has offered up this debate as a palliative in order to soften the image of the Islamic Republic. These critics argue that the very idea of civil society, an unmistakably Western and liberal concept, is incompatible with an Islamic polity, and is a contradiction in terms. And yet the idea of civil society has moved to the center-stage of political discourse in Iran today. Iranians rightly believe that they are witnessing a most fateful turning point in the history of their nation. Civil society activists including women's groups, youth and students, intellectuals and some workers' groups represent a wide spectrum of ideologies, tactics and demands. Some are seeking a few minor changes, others seek serious reforms within the existing system, and some groups want an immediate end to the regime through a revolution.

DOI: 10.1057/9781137330178

There is common agreement among the demonstrators and civil activists that the main contradiction in contemporary Iran is the one between authoritarian violence and democratic nonviolence. This is due to the fact that the protest movement in Iran is nonviolent and civil in its methods of creating social change while also seeking an ethical dimension to Iranian politics. This judgment implies that Iranian civil society is ready to make a distinction between two approaches: searching for truth and solidarity versus lying and using violence. Today young Iranians couch their conversations about politics in a moral vocabulary. Looked at from the Iranian context, civil society is not a homogeneous entity. More than a "voluntary sector" or a "charity sector," it is an "ethical sector." As a matter of fact, talking about civil society in the context of a theocracy like Iran comes to speak of a society of citizens as opposed to a society organized on the grounds of fanatic religiosity. In the Iranian context the obvious question is: what political culture has been the most conducive to the development of civil society? It is certainly not a religious culture, nor necessarily a secular one. But it is certainly a nonviolent and anti-sectarian one. That is to say, the conditions for the formation and consolidation of a civil society in a fundamentalist society like Iran have been threefold. First, there has been a great effort on the issue of "publicity," in the domain of what citizens know about public life. The struggle of independent journalists to create monthly magazines and daily journals in order to inform citizens, not only about local conditions, institutions and interests but also about the government, has been one of the pillars of the Iranian civil society. Second, on the ethical side there has been the effort of Iranian intellectuals to defend the truth against lies and to promote the ethical and political capacity to pass judgment on those who are responsible for the conduct of what falls into the public domain. Finally, the third pillar has been the horizontal relationship of cooperation and mutual support instead of tension and conflict among Iranian women as principal actors of the Iranian civil society.

Factionalism at the top of the Iranian political hierarchy allowed the rest of the society to find spaces to engage in politics. People who were not part of the leadership – young people, university students, intellectuals and women activists – could delve into politics precisely because politics at the top were so openly fractious. The tumult in the parliament during the Khatami presidency and the daily battles among those running the country emboldened people to criticize and even resist the authorities. Had there been a solid consolidation of power and ideological coherence

DOI: 10.1057/9781137330178

at the top, such spaces would not have been opened and such resistance would not have been possible. This is how the idea of civil society penetrated the day-to-day politics of the country, in the slogans of candidates for various offices and especially in the discourse of Mohammad Khatami and his group of followers in the late 1990s.

Three principal positions have emerged in the civil society debate now raging in Iran. First, there are those who regard the whole concept as antithetical to the basic values and ideals of an Islamic society and state. These are the hard-line conservatives, who occupy the most powerful positions within Iran's political establishment. They control all the means of violence in Iranian society (the Revolutionary Guards, the security services, the Basij), and hold much of the economic power as well. The best manifestation of such power was exemplified in Ayatollah Khamenei's discourse during the shutdown of 18 pro-reform publications in April 2000. Following a debate at the Iranian parliament, Khamenei immediately intervened and put an end to the debates by minimizing the role of civil society. "Should the enemies of Islam, the revolution and the Islamic system take over or infiltrate the press, a great danger would threaten the security, unity and the faith of the people, and therefore, I cannot allow myself to keep quiet in this crucial issue," he stated.[1] Three years before this incident, the deputy of the IRGC (Islamic Revolutionary Guards Corps), Mohammad Baqer Zolqadr, had made a powerful move against reformism in Iran marking his violent intention to fully enter the factional battleground: "IRGC will react swiftly to anything that would threaten this holy regime."[2] This violent discourse was completed by a philosophical one which formulated its attack against civil society and democracy as a religious rhetoric against modernity. This was no accident. From the very beginning of the Iranian revolution of 1979, the followers of Ahmad Fardid, an oral philosopher who served during the second Pahlavi era as a leading authority on the philosophy of Martin Heidegger, represented by Reza Davari Ardekani, joined their critique of Western humanism to the critique of nonviolence and democracy by conservative forces. "Humanism has been the pivotal axis of Western history,"[3] commented Davari. He added elsewhere, "Modernity is a tree that was planted in the West and has spread everywhere. For many years we have been living under one of the dying and faded branches of this tree and its dried shadow, which is still hanging over our heads. Although we have taken refuge in Islam, the shadow of this branch has still not yet totally

DOI: 10.1057/9781137330178

disappeared from over our heads. In fact, neither we nor it have left each other alone. What can be done with this dried branch?"[4]

The second group consists of those who want to Islamicize the idea of civil society, to make it compatible with the existing norms and values of the present order. They advocate an "Islamic civil society" that would be clearly distinguishable from its secular, Western counterparts. The call for civil society has been among the key ideas of those who have come to be known as religious intellectuals (*roshanfekran dini*) in Iran in the past decade. In calling for the political participation of Islam and Muslims in civil society rather than their absence from public sphere, Iranian religious intellectuals have clearly reflected a desire to find an alternative to the unending clash between fundamentalist practices and relentless westernization.

> Soon after the landslide victory of the reformists on 23 May 1997 election – referred to in Iran as *Nahzat-e Dowom-e Khordad* – *Jame'eh*, the first reformist paper of its kind, was published by two close associates of Soroush: Mahmoud Sahmsolwaezin, the editor in chief of *Kiyan*, and Mohsen Sazgara, another influential member of the Kiyan circle. Akbar Ganji, a disciple of Soroush and the director of his publishing house, began his journalistic activities and published the new weekly paper of *Rah-e Naw*. It was no wonder that these individuals and many others like them became the promoters of President Khatami's program for "political development" (*tawse'eh siyasi*). In the absence of political parties in the Islamic Republic, the intellectual circles and journals such as *Kiyan* had functioned as quasi-political parties preparing the intellectual foundation and a discourse for political change. The reformist press that grew under Khatami – thanks to the open-mindedness of his first minister of the Department of Culture and Islamic Guidance, Ata'ollah Mohajerani, who issued publishing licenses for reformists – simply carried on the task of its small predecessor. The foundation for reformist writing and publishing had already been laid, and there were many religious and political reform issues to fill their pages. Expressions such as "new interpretation of religion"; "different understandings of religion"; "pluralism"; "religious democratic government"; "rationalism"; "people's sovereignty"; "human rights"; "tolerance," and others that had been taboo in the not very distant past, now became very common elements of the reform discourse. Added to these ideas were two slogans of Khatami's government, "the rule of law" and "civil society" that the press disseminated among all sections of society.[5]

It goes without saying that those religious activists and intellectualists, who since the election of Khatami in 1997 argued that there was no

DOI: 10.1057/9781137330178

contradiction between the two concepts of religion and civil society, widened the gap between the two conflicting principles of republicanism and theocracy in Iran; but they also opened the door to the implementation of nonviolent thinking in the Iranian public sphere. For example, Saeed Hajjarian, the former Intelligence Ministry official who functioned as an intellectual advisor to the reformist movement under Khatami, describes civil society as a space of exchange and civic mindedness where independent groups can increase limitations on the state's power. According to him, "It is through civil society that individuals, each with their own unique personalities, learn how to live together and defend their mutual interests. ... It is through civil society that communication spreads and collective wisdom is deepened. ... It is through civil society that mutually beneficial exchanges take place and rational decision-making grows. ... It is through civil society that political pursuits become possible and the foundations for government are laid."[6] Hasan Yusefi Eshkevari, another prominent figure of religious intellectualism, advocates an unconditional rejection of religious violence and argues that democracy is the most appropriate manner to administer Iranian society with. But he also underlines that Islam has no monopoly on truth. "As a Muslim," he maintains, "I know that my religion is more just and more complete. But I do not have a monopoly over truth and I do not seek to monopolize others. In this sense I am pluralist. I also believe in dialogue, discourse, and mutual understanding among religions, and reject religious violence and force and compulsion, and in this sense I am pluralist as well."[7] It is noteworthy that the former President Khatami also underlined the importance of pluralism in his reformist discourses and actions, but according to Fatemeh Haghighatjoo, a former female deputy in the Iranian parliament, "Khatami raised awareness about the negative cultural characteristics of Iranian society, and brought to the fore such concepts as patience, tolerance, dialogue, questioning and answering, mutual respect and democratic family relations."[8]

Third and in contradistinction to the second group, there are those among secular intellectuals and political activists who view the concept of "civil society" as nonreligious and ideologically neutral in terms of the ultimate goals and values of society, but useful as a basis for structuring state-society relations, protecting the relative autonomy and freedom of citizens and their associations, and promoting a more tolerant, pluralistic and democratic order. Post-revolutionary Iranian civil society is symbolized today, from this point of view, by a period of transition

DOI: 10.1057/9781137330178

from utopian thinking and a quest for an "ideological modernity" to a nonimitative dialogical exchange with modernity. Taken as the capacity for choice among different alternatives, negative liberty has become the central framework for a plural view of Iranian history where teleological and deterministic perspectives are replaced by the adoption of a self-creative perspective through choice-making. The centrality accorded to the activity of choice in the constitution of the new Iranian public space reveals once again the affinities of this generation of intellectuals and activists with the ideals of rational autonomy and value-pluralism, as opposed to the applications of monistic ideas in the Iranian social and political realm by the previous generations. The central point here is that this third group of civil society activists has come to think of Iranian civil society in a different way, not only as individuals but also as a generation. Looked at more closely it becomes clearer that these intellectuals and activists have been marked by one big event: the emergence of the Iranian Revolution of 1979 and the violence it engendered. Like a wall of water crashing against the shore, revolutionary violence disintegrated in the souls of these intellectuals and activists, leaving them with the difficult task of living up to and thinking about what was happening in them and through them. More than 30 years later their distinctive contribution to the Iranian political debate is not how to choose between morality and politics, in a society where cynicism and confusion cover the voices of common sense and civility, but how to forge a politics of responsibility and nonviolence, in the absence of which only silence and untruth would reign.

A discussion of nonviolent discourse in Iranian civil society by intellectuals and social activists would be somewhat incomplete without the mention of women's rights movement and its struggle for nonviolence. For more than 30 years, the women's rights movement has been at the forefront in the struggle for human rights and gender equality in Iran and as such it has been crucial to the overall struggle for democracy and nonviolence in Iran. Iranian women have bravely resisted in a nonviolent manner over and over to end gender-based discrimination, only to be met with extreme violence such as beatings, arrests and imprisonment of activists. These collective attempts, together with the smaller ones, resulted in cooperation among different generations of Iranian women to challenge the discrimination prescribed in Iran's legal code. While the women's movement is nonhomogeneous and lacks the necessary coordination and well-defined political goals beside the aim of gender

DOI: 10.1057/9781137330178

equality, it remains an important catalyst for nonviolent mobilization in Iran. Paradoxically, the creation of a theocratic state in 1979 – undermining the rights of women, segregating public and educational spheres and implementing orthodox Islamic rules in civil and criminal rights against women – paved the way for the massive participation of women in the Iranian public sphere. For three decades Iranian women have gradually empowered their position in the Iranian public sphere by making themselves visible through the enhancement of educational, communication and virtual spheres and by challenging gender structures of the Iranian society and offering nonviolent gender patterns. Production of new feminist discourses within the Iranian women's rights movement has reinforced the nonviolent role of Iranian women against unjust and disempowering structures while establishing a critical front against neo-fundamentalist discourses and practices.

The ultimate expression of such an empowerment became evident in the collective and united action of Iranian women in the campaign to collect One Million Signatures to Change Discriminatory Laws. This campaign was an important step for the equality of rights between women and men in Iranian laws, but it was certainly a giant leap for nonviolent action in Iran. In January 2009, the campaign was awarded the Simone De Beauvoir Prize for Women's Freedom in recognition of its significant impact on Iranian society. However, many women activists have been arrested in the past few years for their involvement in the One Million Signatures campaign. If anything, women in Iran have challenged vehemently the patriarchal structures and the violent attitudes in Iranian public sphere. As Noushin Ahmadi Khorasani, a women's rights campaigner and journalist points out, "If we have all decided to go towards democracy and equality, it is absolutely necessary to overcome the old traditions and ideologies, in particular to end the monistic culture (even when we are being suppressed) and not put all our eggs in the basket of politics and governmental religion. Hence all of us, the Iranians can help one another to reach our democratic objective, peacefully and non violent, and through processes we can institutionalize them."[9] What is unprecedented here is not only the fact that women from all walks of life have taken part in the Iranian women's rights movement but also that they are rallied behind nonviolent, nonideological and pro-democracy ideals rather than utopian, sectarian and revolutionary discourses. One can add that Iranian women have welcomed the discourse of nonviolence as a means for their empowerment in Iranian civil society and a strategy

DOI: 10.1057/9781137330178

for the elimination of gender inequalities and violence against them. The re-affirmation and the reinforcement of the concept of nonviolence by Iranian women has opened the doors of a meaningful dialogue among themselves and with Iranian men, while refusing to enter the vicious culture of violence which is perpetuated by the Islamic regime in Iran. This new level of public consciousness has repeatedly reminded the sociological actors of the Iranian civil society that the struggle for democracy in Iran cannot be defined solely by the struggle against theocratic structure, the supremacy of the clerical power in politics, and the absolute rule of the jurist (*velayat-e motlaqeh faqih*) but mainly in opposition to the dominant mindset of power accumulation and violence in Iranian society.

The prevalence of nonviolence, especially the choice of civil disobedience and a silent demonstration as a unifying movement, gave the Iranian civil society a sort of "Gandhian" tone. This rather spiritual and peaceful mood that predominated because of the presence of many Iranian women, especially young women, continued during the first months of protests in the aftermath of the Presidential elections of June 2009. The massive public demonstrations of June 2009 in Iran, unprecedented since the revolution of 1979, should be considered more as a main contradiction in contemporary Iran between authoritarian violence and democratic nonviolence than a battle between the supporters of Mir-Hossein Mousavi, the reformist challenger and Mahmoud Ahmadinejad, the incumbent president. It is actually a dialectic between the powerless nonviolent truth-seekers on the one hand, and powerful lie-makers and users of violence on the other hand. With that said, an equally important fact is that most of the young demonstrators who have been questioning the legitimacy of Iran's electoral process and now the credibility of the Iranian political institutions are not, unlike their parents, interested in revolutionary upheaval or violent change. Some could be prepared to take their protests to the limit. Many others, however, have no interest in an all-out violence against the country's Islamic system. It is interesting up to what point the unarmed and peaceful Iranians across all ages and classes flocked to the streets of Tehran and other cities defying brutal paramilitary squads, and to demand major transformations in the structure of the political establishment in Iran. One of the main characteristics of this civic movement was to pledge to continue a peaceful struggle for democracy in Iran, leading itself through a network structure which spread from certain neighborhoods to other neighborhoods, from the university students to the high-school students, from

DOI: 10.1057/9781137330178

the technologically savvy youth to their parents, from the big cities to smaller cities, and from the members of the middle class to those of the working class. The spontaneity and self-motivation of this movement stemmed from the fact that the people came, for the first time, to feel strongly and instinctively about their citizenship rights as something worth sacrificing for.

Today, the Iranian civic movement claims to be the carrier of a momentous change in Iran. It expresses hope that its success would bring democracy and respect of human rights in Iran. But the realization of the goals of this movement is not easy and may not be achieved in the short term. More close contacts between Iranians inside and the large Iranian population in Diaspora could also enhance the nonviolent skills of the movement and bring up questions about the formulation of its long-term strategy. Although it is true that the popular demonstrations did not bring an end to the Iranian regime, their consequences damaged the regime's domestic and international legitimacy. The diminishing number of protestors in the streets of Tehran gives the impression that the protest movement is fading away and that Mr. Mousavi and Mr. Karroubi are losing steam. For these two opposition leaders the choice is whether to accept a humiliating deal with Ahmadinejad's government that would greatly diminish their moral and political statures. As for the Iranian authorities the question is still whether the continuous crackdowns have succeeded in putting an end to the popular quest for democracy in Iran or on the contrary have provoked a wider challenge to their rule. As such, the emerging power dynamics leave Iranian Green Movement dissidents with tough choices. If they continue informing the Iranian rulers of their lawful rights through nonviolent demonstrations they would certainly increase the influence of the military and security forces and risk bloodshed, but if they put an end to their movement of civil disobedience because of the harsh repression in the past year they might lose the support and sympathy of the outside world. This means that while the Iranian political structure has been going through a crisis of legitimacy and current power holders have lost moral credibility by virtue of cruelty and lying in politics, the Iranian civil society has redefined its legitimacy by re-founding and refining its republican principles. Thus the republican gesture in Iran continues to pay attention almost exclusively to the legitimacy of the public space in opposition to the political theology that is represented and expressed by the absolute sovereignty of the leader of the Revolution. The Iranian public space is faced, then, with the problem of

DOI: 10.1057/9781137330178

combining a rejection of absolute sovereignty with the need to put faith in a challenge "from below" – in the independent life of civil society outside the frame of state power. This, of course, resides in the self-organization of Iranian civil society that defies the violence embodied in the Iranian state and its instruments of control and domination. But it is also closely related to new ethical standards against which Iranian political reality could be measured. By assuming an ethical stance the Iranian civil society can make a stronger political case.

In a violent political society like Iran in which most of the ethical values have been largely discarded the choice of nonviolent action by the Iranian Green Movement is a proof of its political maturity and moral integrity. A year of extraordinary cruelty has passed and no one has been held accountable by the international public opinion for extreme violence against Iranian citizens. As such, perhaps the first step to help Iran's quest for democracy is to acknowledge and encourage dissident voices inside and outside Iran while keeping human rights issues high on the agenda. As the international community focuses on Iran's nuclear program, it should also focus on the violation of human rights in Iran as a matter of urgency. The fact that more sanctions are needed against Iran is a secondary issue. What is needed now is courage to challenge the moral and political illegitimacy of state violence in Iran. To this end, it is important to have solidarity from other citizens of the world in supporting the Iranian struggle for respect of universal values of human rights.

The true hero of the Iranian civic movement is the emerging model of nonviolent resistance that provides the clearest guideline and vision for Iran's gradual transition to democracy. Today the most difficult challenge of Iranian civil society is to face the violence of the dominant political system without losing its hope. Many analysts believe that this is not possible. That might be the case. But after a year of extreme hardship hope is the only pillar that holds up the Iranian civic movement. Hope is the future of a democratic Iran. What is certain is that this hope is closely bound to a silent nonviolent revolution underway in Iran today.

Notes

1   *Voice of the Islamic Republic*, Radio 1, Tehran, August 6, 2000, quoted in Ghoncheh Tazmini, *Khatami's Iran: The Islamic Republic and the Turbulent Path to Reform*, London: I.B. Tauris Publishers, 2009, p. 110.

DOI: 10.1057/9781137330178

2 *Kayhan* (November 15, 1997), quoted in Tazmini, *Khatami's Iran*, p. 107.

3 Quoted in Mehran Kamrava, *Iran's Intellectual Revolution*, New York: Cambridge University Press, 2008, p. 65.

4 Reza Davari Ardakani, *Enqelab-e Eslami va Vaz-e Konuni-ye Alam* (*Islamic Revolution and the Present Status of the World*), Tehran, Entesharat-e Markaz-e Farhangi-ye Allameh Tabatabai, 1983, p. 83, quoted in Tazmini, *Khatami's Iran*, p.118.

5 Emphasis added. Forough Jahanbakhsh, "Religious and Political Discourse in Iran: Moving Toward Post-Fundamentalism" *The Brown Journal of World Affairs*, Vol. IX, no. 2 (Winter/Spring 2003): 250–251.

6 Saeed Hajjarian, *Jomhuriyyat; Afsonzodai az Qodrat* (*Republicanism, Demystification of Power*), Tehran: Tarh-e No, (1379/2000): 355–356, quoted in Mehran Kamrava, *Iran's Intellectual Revolution*, New York: Cambridge University Press, 2008, p. 142.

7 Hassan Yusefi Eshkevari, *Ta'amollat-e Tanha-ee: Dibacheh-ee bar Hermeneutic-e Irani* (*Thoughts in Solitude: An Introduction to Iranian Hermeneutics*) Tehran, Saraee, (1382/2003): 147–48, quoted in Kamrava, *Iran's Intellectual Revolution*, p. 136.

8 Quoted in Tazmini, *Khatami's Iran*, p. 137.

9 Quoted in http://iranfemschool.com/english/spip.php?article368

DOI: 10.1057/9781137330178

Epilogue

Abstract: *Iran's traumatic experiences with undemocratic violence and especially in the contemporary period have developed a nonviolent and democratic conscience among the younger generation of Iranians. The relevance of nonviolence in Iran is still robust, for Iranians are not yet rid of undemocratic institutions that resist democracy. However, one of the lessons that Iranian civic actors seem to have retained from their recent political history is that violence, either religious or secular, has been a complete and enduring failure in establishing democracy in Iran.*

Jahanbegloo, Ramin. *Democracy in Iran*. Basingstoke: Palgrave Macmillan, 2013. DOI: 10.1057/9781137330178.

DOI: 10.1057/9781137330178

As an exercise in Iranian political history and the theory of democracy, this study has employed a bipartite approach which brings together a working hypothesis with recognition of historical particularity. It is only by combining these two that one can begin properly to analyze and appreciate the process of taming violence in contemporary Iranian politics.

The working hypothesis was based on the assumption that Iran's traumatic experiences with undemocratic violence over centuries and especially since the Iranian revolution of 1906 have served as the catalyst for its democratic conscientization. Political violence in Iran has compelled Iranians to confront fundamental questions about being Iranian, to ask what is central to Iranian identity. In particular, the recent experience of violence during the post-electoral period of June 2009 forced Iranians to ask what binds them together and constitutes their essential unity. Iranians soon realized that their political and cultural heritage constitutes a constant source of conflict. The question of what should constitute today's Iranian identity remains contested.

The Constitutionalists of 1906–1911 appeared as a curious amalgam of modernists asking for practical and lawful changes and Islamic nationalists who wanted the end of foreign rule while looking for an ideological synonymity between Shi'ism and Persianness. As for the first and second Pahlavi regimes, they used Iranian nationalist discourse to form a centralized and modernized state, while leaving many traditional and religious questions unanswered. The Persianization of the state with a focus on pre-Islamic Iran and its imperial grandeur was a major feature of government policies during the Pahlavis. In the Shah's own words, Iran was going toward the Great Civilization which he defined as an achievable project: "A highly humanitarian and democratic social order will prevail in Iran during the era of the Great Civilization, with individual freedoms, social justice, economic democracy, decentralization, informed public participation in all affairs, and productive national culture."[1] By mid-1979 the new Islamic regime installed on the ruins of the Shah's Great Civilization would redefine Iran and Iranian identity as fully Islamic, institutionalizing the authority of the Shi'ite jurists and including the concept of *velayat-e faqih* at the centre of Iranian Constitution. This redefinition of Iranian identity accompanied with a great movement of violence also served to exclude all the other "non-Islamic" and "non-revolutionary" social elements from the mainstream of political and cultural life. Therefore, the emphasis on the Islamic

DOI: 10.1057/9781137330178

heritage of Iranian identity relegated the modern narrative to the margins.

Herein lies the main Gordian knot to the question of violence in contemporary Iran. The question to ask is that of reconciliation among the three distinctive ontological, anthropological and political layers of Iranian identity, meaning the pre-Islamic, Islamic and modern historical experiences in Iran. As Abdolkarim Soroush points out, "The three cultures that form our common heritage era are of national, religious and Western origins. While steeped in an ancient national culture, we are also immersed in our religious culture, and we are at the same time awash in successive waves coming from the Western shores. Whatever solutions that we divine for our problems must come from this mixed heritage to which our contemporary social thinkers, reformers and modernizers have been heirs, often seeking the salvation of our people in the hegemony of one of these cultures over the other two."[2] Although perfect reconciliation among these three cultures is impossible, lack of effort and progress is inexcusable, because it will result in greater violence in the future of Iran. To engage in nonviolent politics means the impossibility of finding perfect solutions; hence there will always be a price to pay. What remains essential here is a new culture of citizenship in Iran liberating itself from a monolithic and closed discourse that denies plural ways of discovering and building truth. Diversity and openness are the two keys to the survival of Iranian civil society and its nonviolent nature. Therefore, it goes against the very nature of Iranian civil society to favor sectarian conceptions of society, be they the ideals of republicanism, secularism or democracy. On this view, the future success of nonviolence in Iranian civil society will draw upon the level of plurality of views, even those which reject nonviolence as an idealistic and irrational solution to the progress of Iran. That is why the only place to which Iranian citizens should return is the here and now. Starting from the realities of the present and simultaneously looking into Iranian past, a new ethical vision might yet emerge, which is that of forgiveness.

At the same time, the aim of this study has been to show that any nation, like Iran, which is in the process of healing its structural violence is confronted with moral and political questions about accountability for criminal actions and atrocities that were once legalized as government policy. At some point in the future Iranians have to decide what should be done with the secret police, torturers, informers and collaborators from the previous regime. Should they be hunted down? Should they

DOI: 10.1057/9781137330178

be exposed? Should they be made accountable? And should they be punished? Or should we let old wounds heal in order to achieve national reconciliation? Recovering the past records of atrocities presents many levels of difficulty, especially when a society finds a strong interest in preserving itself through lies. There is a standard rhetoric of governmental or national responses to allegations of human rights violations. This rhetoric usually contains several elements like: "There was no rape or torture of prisoners, these are lies because people like us don't do things like that" or "Talking about violence in Iran is a British, American or Zionist conspiracy" and finally the most standard response is to say that: "Tortures and killings were justified in the name of God or for the revolution or in defense of national security." However, the most profound and genuine obstacle to accountability is raised by the issues of authority, responsibility and obedience to orders as it was the case for the Nazi criminals. The reference to accountability in society like Iran is closely related to a process of shaming or removing previous wrong doings. But even if rituals of expiation are initiated and completed, this will not necessarily eradicate the moral conditions which gave rise to gross abuse of human rights. For this reason, in the case of Iran two things should be taken into consideration. The first is to address the whole base of civil society and its role in the process of taming violence. Second, and more important, is to make the whole Iranian society accountable, and not only the offenders with how knowledge of repression was and is represented and how the structures of violence were and are accepted in the Iranian society.

We can make here a comparative analysis of the concept of "Iranian guilt" with what the German philosopher, Karl Jaspers, called "The Question of German Guilt." Jaspers very correctly stressed the importance of prosecuting Nazi war criminals as an element in a more general re-evaluation of responsibility after Nazism. He argued that the Nuremberg trials made a necessary distinction between those who were criminally guilty and the indefinite number of others who were capable of cooperating with Nazism under orders. Jaspers rejected the defenses advanced by the Nazi defendants as an evasion of their responsibility because, as he said, the institution of crimes against humanity is based not only on the political structures in which violations of human rights happen, but also on the moral responsibility of a nation in its tiny acts of indifference which make injustice and crime possible. As such, when the machinery of state crime and state murder makes practically everyone

DOI: 10.1057/9781137330178

complicit, by replacing the ethical foundations of a society with structures of discursive and public violence, then the visible signs of distinction between the guilty and the innocent are effaced. Also, when people are prepared to do their jobs as cogs in a murdering machine and see themselves simply as doing their job without responsibility for the consequences of their actions, they do not regard themselves as murderers because they kill only in a professional capacity. We can call this not only an evasion of responsibility, but also a strategy to normalize atrocities as normal routines of power holding. In the Iranian case, as in the German case, we need to go beyond this argument presented by Robert Servatius, Adolf Eichmann's lawyer, making an equation between "acts for which you are decorated if you win and go to gallows if you lose."[3] Actually, Eichmann's claim to have been just following orders was not an acceptable defense, either before an international court, or before human conscience. This would be the case for those who have committed crimes in the name of the Islamic regime. Their crimes are those against humanity, not simply Iranians.

History may never uncover exactly what brought the Iranian nation to the point of wholeheartedly accepting the Islamic regime in 1979. But it will certainly admire those who followed the law of their conscience regardless of the written law they lived under and refused to be estranged from themselves as well as from others and from the world. Many Iranians, probably even those among the civil servants and simple peasants, refused to murder, to rob and to let their neighbors go off to prison or death. God knows how they learned to resist temptation, but they certainly represent an ethic of responsibility and an ongoing exercise of ethical judgment in the face of violence. In this line of thought, clichés about "turning a new page" must be placed in their moral and political contexts. The more principled appeals for reconciliation or forgiveness do not call for any denial of the past or an evasion of responsibility. On the contrary, they depend on a full acknowledgment of events. According to Paul Ricoeur, forgiveness is not a kind of forgetting "which would signify a retrospective approbation regarding the evil done."[4] But it is, nevertheless, an important moral action in uprooting the structures of violence in a society like Iran. The danger in countries like Iran is that punishment always remains imprisoned within the repetition of vengeance. We should not make a banal cliché out of the concept of forgiveness. Forgiveness does not mean "doing nothing." Just as Nazi atrocities cannot be reconciled by crying for the ashes of those who

DOI: 10.1057/9781137330178

perished in concentration camps, in the same way we cannot forget to hold accountable those who have been responsible for the torture and massacre of thousands of Iranians during the past 30 years in Iran. Efforts to repair victims of violence in Iran must, therefore, be seen as an essential element of an international justice package, precisely because reparations constitute a form of recognition that all Iranian citizens owe to those whose fundamental rights have been violated in Iran.

It has also been argued that in dealing with this process of change, we are constantly reminded of the Gandhian dilemma of reconciling nonviolent principles with political power. If this is true, then violence ceases to serve as a meaningful and instrumental concept in the process of accountability for perpetrators of crimes against humanity in Iran. In that case, re-establishing trust among Iranian citizens by eliminating the fear of living together necessitates a moral condemnation of violence in Iranian society. It is this very emphasis on the taming of violence that gives Gandhi's theory of nonviolence all its moral authority and political relevance in Iran today. The relevance of nonviolence in Iran for our new century is still robust, for Iranians are not yet rid of rulers who resist democracy. The world in which Iranians try to survive is far different from that of Gandhi, but in the life of a nation that is struggling for democracy, nonviolent sanction is frequently in use. Every time a civil society movement confronts a tyrannical government in Iran, nonviolent action is back in a struggle that tries to end oppression and establish democracy. New reasons for using nonviolent action may also develop as the civil dynamism in Iran is able to convince new generations of Iranians to evaluate morally and politically their choice of nonviolence and come to appreciate democratic order as best serving their interests. One of the lessons that Iranian people seem to have retained from their recent political history is that violence, either religious or secular, has been a complete and enduring failure in establishing democracy in Iran. The violence of religious fanatics and the violence of secular fanatics in Iran seem to be two faces of the same coin. Both sides claim that Iranian people are on their side, but the issue is whether they are on the side of Iranian people. It goes without saying that in the light of Iranian contemporary history, it is getting ever more difficult to argue that violence benefits the people in this region of the world. One could argue that it has been ideological and religious violence which have consistently undermined Iran's democratic development. In other words, a fear of

DOI: 10.1057/9781137330178

the other has helped violence to have claims upon the political function of Iranian society. If each side has refused to understand the other, it is because each side has seen itself only as a victim and not as an executioner. A sense of victimization has been accompanied on each side with a justification and legitimization of violence.

But how can we get out of this cycle of violence and how can the Iranians reverse the direction of violence and start looking toward their nonviolent and democratic future? No realist would believe today in any brilliant formula that will immediately end violence in Iran. This might be true; but the 20th century is gone, and the 21st century is a challenging one for Iranians. Iran is caught in a dilemma. If it does not end its culture of violence, not only as a state but also as a society, it will lose both its integrity as an old civilization that still has something to offer to the world and its future as a democratic state in the Middle East. Never has any such choice stemming from the potentials of the new generations in Iran been so inevitable yet so completely uncertain.

Notes

1   M.R. Pahlavi, *Be Sooye Tamadun-e Bozorg*, p. 279, quoted in Ali M. Ansari, *Modern Iran: The Pahlavis and After*, Essex: Pearson Education Limited, 2007, p. 239.

2   A. Soroush, *Reason, Freedom and Democracy in Islam*, trans. and ed. M. Sadri and A. Sadri Oxford: Oxford University Press, 2000, p. 156.

3   Hannah Arendt, *Eichmann in Jerusalem; A Report on the Banality of Evil*, New York: Penguin Books, 1977, pp. 21–22.

4   Quoted in Gil Anidjar, "Memory, History, Forgiveness: A Dialogue Between Paul Ricoeur and Sorin Antohi," *Janus Head* 8 (2005): 14–25.

DOI: 10.1057/9781137330178

Bibliography

Abrahamian, Ervand. *Iran between Two Revolutions.*
Princeton: Princeton University Press, 1983.

Abrahamian, Ervand. "The Causes of the Constitutional
Revolution in Iran." *International Journal of Middle East
Studies* 10 (1979): 381–414.

Abrahamian, Ervand. "The Crowd in the Persian
Revolution." *Iranian Studies* 2 (1969): 128–150.

Adamiyat, Fereydoun. *Fekr-e Demokrasi-ye Ejtema'i
dar Nehzat-e Mashrutiyat-e Iran (The Idea of Social
Democracy in the Constitutional Movement of Iran).*
Tehran, 1976.

Adamiyat, Fereydoun. *Fekr-e Azadi va Moqaddameh-ye
Nehzat-e Mashroutiyat-e Iran* [*The Idea of Liberty and
the Beginning of the Iranian Constitutional Movement*].
Tehran, 1961–1962.

Afshar, Haleh. *Iran: A Revolution in Turmoil.* London:
Macmillan Press, 1985.

Afary, Janet. *The Iranian Constitutional Revolution,
1906–1911: Grassroots Democracy, Social Democracy
and the Origins of Feminism.* New York: Columbia
University Press,1996.

Akhundzadeh, Mirza Fath Ali. *Maktubat*, ed. M. Subhdam.
Dusseldorf, Germany: Mard-i-Imruz, 1985.

Algar, Hamid. (trans.) *Islam and Revolution: Writings and
Declarations of Imam Khomeini.* Berkeley: Mizan Press,
1981.

Algar, Hamid. *Mirza Malkum Khan: A Study in the History
of Iranian Modernism.* London: University of California
Press, 1973.

DOI: 10.1057/9781137330178

Al-Ahmad, Jalal. *Occidentosis: A Plague from the West*. Translated by R. Campbell. Berkeley: Mizan Press, 1984.

Amuzegar, Jahangir. *The Dynamics of the Iranian Revolution: The Pahlavis' Triumph and Tragedy*. New York: State University of New York Press, 1991.

Anidjar, Gill. "Memory, History, Forgiveness: A Dialogue Between Paul Ricoeur and Sorin Antohi." *Janus Head* 8 (2005): 14–25.

Ansari, Ali M. *Modern Iran: The Pahlavis and After*. Essex, UK: Pearson Education Limited, 2007.

Arendt, Hannah. *Eichmann in Jerusalem: A Report on the Banality of Evil*. New York: Penguin Books, 1977.

Arendt, Hannah. *On Violence*. New York: Harvest Books, 1970.

Avery, Peter. *Modern Iran*. New York: Frederick A Praeger Publishers, 1965.

Azimi, Fakhreddin. "Unseating Mossadeq: The Configuration and Role of Domestic Forces." In *Mohammad Mossadeq and the 1953 Coup in Iran*, edited by M.J. Gasiorowski and M. Byrne, 27–101. Syracuse: Syracuse University Press, 2004.

Bayat, Mangol. *Iran's First Revolution: Shi'ism and the Constitutional Revolution of 1905–1909*. Oxford: Oxford University Press, 1991.

Bayat-Phillip, Mangol. "Shi'ism in Contemporary Iranian Politics: The Case of Ali Shari'ati." In *Towards a Modern Iran*, edited by Elie Kedourie and Sylvia G. Haim, 64–95. London: Frank Cass, 1980.

Behdad, Sohrab. " Utopia of Assassins: Navvab Safavi and the Feda'ian-e Eslam in Prerevolutionary Iran." In *Iran: Between Tradition and Modernity*, edited by Ramin Jahanbegloo, 71–92. Maryland: Lexington Books, 2004.

Boroujerdi, Mehrzad. *Iranian Intellectuals and the West: The Tormented Triumph of Nativism*. Syracuse: Syracuse University Press, 1996.

Cole, Juan. "Imami Jurisprudence and the Role of the Ulama." In *Religion and Politics in Iran: Shiism from Quietism to Revolution*, edited by Nikki R. Keddie, 33–46. New Haven: Yale University Press, 1983.

Cole, Juan, and Nikki R. Keddie. (eds) *Shi'ism and Social Protest*. New Haven: Yale University Press, 1986.

Cronin, Stephanie. *The Making of Modern Iran: State and Society Under Riza Shah, 1921–1941*. London: Routledge, 2003.

Davis, Simon. *Contested Space: Anglo-American Relations in the Persian Gulf, 1939–1947*. Leiden: Martinus Nijhoff Publishers, 2009.

DOI: 10.1057/9781137330178

Floor, Willem N. "The Revolutionary Character of the Ulama: Wishful Thinking or Reality?" In *Religion and Politics in Iran*, edited by Nikki R. Keddie, 47–72. New Haven: Yale University Press, 1983.

Foran, John. "The Strengths and Weaknesses of Iran's Populist Alliance: A Class Analysis of the Constitutional Revolution of 1905–1911." *Theory and Society*, 20 (1991): 796–823.

Gandhi, MK. *The Collected Works of M.K. Gandhi*. New Delhi, India: The Publications Division, 2010.

Ganji, Akbar. "The Struggle Against Sultanism." *Journal of Democracy* 16 (2005): 38–51.

Gasiorowski, M.J. "Why Did Mossadeq Fall?" In *Mohammad Mossadeq and the 1953 Coup in Iran*, edited by M.J. Gasiorowski and M. Byrne, 227–260. Syracuse: Syracuse University Press, 2004.

Gheissari, Ali, and Vali Nasr. *Democracy in Iran: History and the Quest for Liberty*. Oxford: Oxford University Press, 2006.

Gheissari, Ali. *Iranian Intellectuals in the 20th Century*. Austin: University of Texas Press, 1998.

Ghods, M.R. "Iranian Nationalism and Reza Shah." *Middle Eastern Studies* 27 (1991): 35–45.

Herbert, Thomas. *Travels in Persia, 1617–1629*. Reprinted by The Islamic World in Foreign Travel Accounts, London, 1995.

Hobbes, Thomas. *Leviathan*. Edited by C.B. Macpherson. London: Penguin Books, 1968.

Holakouee-Naeinee, Farhang. *The Constitutional Revolution of Iran, 1906: A Sociological Analysis*. Michigan: Xerox University Microfilms, 1974.

Ibsen, Henrik. *Pillars of Society*. The Gutenberg Project Ebook, 2007. Accessed January 22, 2013, http://www.gutenberg.org/files/2296/2296. txt.

Islamic Republic of Iranian Constitution. Accessed January 19, 2012, http://www.iranonline.com/iran/iran-info/Government/constitution.html

Irfani, Suroosh. *Revolutionary Islam in Iran*. London: Zed Books, 1983.

Jahanbakhsh, Forough. "Religious and Political Discourse in Iran: Moving Toward Post Fundamentalism." *The Brown Journal of World Affairs* IX (2003): 243–254.

Kane, John. *The Politics of Moral Capital*. New York: Cambridge University Press, 2001.

Kamrava, Mehran. *Iran's Intellectual Revolution*. New York: Cambridge University Press, 2008.

DOI: 10.1057/9781137330178

Katouzian, Homa. "Mossadeq's Government in Iranian History:
Arbitrary Rule, Democracy and the 1953 Coup." In *Mohammad
Mossadeq and the 1953 Coup in Iran*, edited by M.J. Gasiorowski
and M. Byrne, 1–26. Syracuse: Syracuse University Press, 2004.

Katouzian, Homa. *Iranian History and Politics: The Dialectic of State and
Society*. London: Routledge, 2003.

Katouzian, Homa. *Mussadiq and the Struggle for Power in Iran*. London:
I.B.Tauris, 1990.

Keddie, Nikki R. *Modern Iran: Roots and Results of Revolution*. New
Haven: Yale University Press, 2006.

Keddie, Nikki R. *Iran and the Muslim World: Resistance and Revolution*.
New York: New York University Press, 1995.

Keddie, Nikkie R. *Religion and Politics in Iran: Shi'ism from Quietism to
Revolution*. New Haven: Yale University Press, 1983.

Khomeini, R. *Islam and Revolution: Writing and Declarations of
Imam Khomeini*, ed. and trans. Hamid Algar. Berkeley: Mizan
Press, 1981.

Khomeini, R. "The Granting of Capitulatory Rights to the US." In *Islam
and Revolution: Writings and Declarations of Imam Khomeini*, Algar, H.
(trans.), 181–188. Berkeley: Mizan Press, 1981.

Kia, Mehrdad. "Constitutionalism, Economic Modernization and Islam
in the Writings of Mirza Yusef Khan Mostashar od-Dowle." *Middle
Eastern Studies* 30 (1994): 751–777.

Lambton, A.K.S. *Qajar Persia: Eleven Studies*. London: I.B.Tauris,
1987.

Lenczowski, George. *Iran Under the Pahlavis*. Stanford: Hoover
institution Press, 1978.

Mackey, Sandra. *The Iranians*. New York: Plume, 1988.

Marbury, Efimenco, N. "An Experiment with Civilian Dictatorship in
Iran: The Case of Mohammed Mossadegh." *The Journal of Politics* 17
(1955): 390–406.

Masroori, Cyrus. "European Thought in Nineteenth-Century Iran:
David Hume and Others." *Journal of the History of Ideas* 61 (2000):
657–674.

Manzoor, Parvez S. *The Sovereignty of the Political: Carl Schmitt
and the Nemesis of Liberalism*. Accessed January 22, 2013, http://
evansexperientialism.freewebspace.com/carlschmitte.htm

Martin, Vanessa. *Creating an Islamic State: Khomeini and the Making of a
New Iran*. London: I.B.Tauris, 2000.

DOI: 10.1057/9781137330178

McCormick, John P. "Fear, Technology, and the State: Carl Schmitt, Leo Strauss, and the Revival of Hobbes in Weimar and National Socialist Germany." *Political Theory* 22 (1994): 619–652.

Mirsepassi, Ali. *Intellectual Discourse and the Politics of Modernization: Negotiating Modernity in Iran.* Cambridge: Cambridge University Press, 2000.

Mohammadi, Majid. *Judicial Reform and Reorganization in 20th Century Iran: State Building, Modernization and Islamicization.* New York: Routledge, 2008.

Mozzafari, Mehdi. "Why the Bazaar Rebels." *Journal of Peace Research* 28 (1991): 377–391.

Nabavi, Negin. "The Discourse of 'Authentic Culture' in Iran in the 1960s and 1970s." In *Intellectual Trends in Twentieth-Century Iran: A Critical Survey*, edited by Negin Nabavi, 91–110. Miami: University Press of Florida, 2003.

Nashat, Guit. *The Origins of Modern Reform in Iran, 1870–1880.* Chicago: University of Illinois Press, 1982.

Pal, Amitabh. *Islamic Nonviolence: The Iranian Example.* The Amana Media Initiative. http://www.arfasia.org/amana/prod/index. php?option=com_content&task=view d=3421&Itemid=98.

Santayana, George. *Life of Reason: Vol.1.* New York: Scribner, 1953.

Schirazi, Asghar. *The Constitution of Iran: Politics and the State in the Islamic Republic.* New York: I.B. Tauris, 1997.

Schmitt, Carl. *Political Theology.* Chicago: University of Chicago Press, 2006.

Soroush, A. *Reason, Freedom and Democracy in Islam.* Translated and edited by M. Sadri and A. Sadri. Oxford: Oxford University Press, 2000.

Steinberger, Peter. "Hobbes, Rousseau and the Modern Conception of the State." *Journal of Politics* 70 (2008): 595–611.

Subhdam, M. (ed.) *Maktubat.* Paris: Mard-i Imruz, 1985.

Summitt, April R. "For a White Revolution: John F. Kennedy and the Shah of Iran." *Middle East Journal* 58 (2004): 560–575.

Tabari, Azar. "The Role of the Clergy in Modern Iranian Politics." In *Religion and Politics in Iran: Shiism from Quietism to Revolution*, edited by Nikki R. Keddie, 47–72. New Haven: Yale University Press, 1983.

Tazmini, Ghoncheh. *Khatami's Iran: The Islamic Republic and the Turbulent Path to Reform.* London: I.B. Tauris Publishers, 2009.

DOI: 10.1057/9781137330178

Tilly, Charles. *Big Structures, Large Processes, Huge Comparisons.* New York: Russell Sage Foundation, 1984.

Travis, John. "Iranian-American Academic Detained in Tehran." *University World News.* August 2, 2009.

van Mill, David. "Hobbes and the Limits of Freedom." Paper prepared for the Australasian Political Studies Association, Canberra, Australia, October 4–6, 2000.

Zubaida, Sami. "An Islamic State? The Case of Iran." *Middle East Report* 153 (1988): 3–7.

DOI: 10.1057/9781137330178

Index

DOI: 10.1057/9781137330178

DOI: 10.1057/9781137330178

CPSIA information can be obtained at www.ICGtesting.com
Printed in the USA
LVOW12*1344130114

369211LV00006B/87/P